If You Can't Climb The Wall, Build A Door!

inti

Publishing

If You Can't Climb The Wall, Build A Door!
Principles To Live By When Quitting Is Not An Option

by Dr. Charles C. Lever

Printed in the United States of America
First Edition, October, 1997

ISBN 0-9632667-7-2

Published by INTI Publishing
Tampa, FL

Cover design by Laurie Winters
Layout by Bayou Graphics

DEDICATION

~

To my wonderful wife, "Sam," whose love and support are a constant source of inspiration to me, and whose life exemplifies the great truth that if you can't climb the wall, then you build a door.

TABLE OF CONTENTS

Dedication iii

Acknowledgments vii

Introduction ix

PART ONE - UP AGAINST THE WALL

CH. 1 Confronting Life's Challenges 3
Building a Sound Foundation... Adversity Comes to All... The Easy Path May Not Be the Best Path... Anticipating Consequences... Using the Mind to Avoid "Mind Fields"... Acting as a Dream Maker, Not a Dream Taker... Review

CH. 2 Living Above Adversity 19
Adversity Changes Our Perceptions... Adversity Brings Out the Best... Adversity Makes Us Stronger... Adversity Opens up New Opportunities... Adversity Compels Us to Change... Adversity Builds Confidence... Review

CH. 3 Moving Beyond A Rock And A Hard Place 33
Avoid The Pitfalls of the Past... Conquer Your Complacency... Acquiesce to Abundance... Review

CH. 4 Capturing The Vision 47
Your Vision: The Gateway to Life... Depth for the Long Haul... Breadth to Avoid Tunnel Vision... Height to Stretch Your Horizons... Count the Cost... Moving Beyond Your Comfort Zone... Courage to Persevere... Review

PART TWO - CLIMBING THE WALL OR BUILDING A DOOR

CH. 5 Positioning Yourself 65
Positioning Our Lives in Relation to Our Goals... In Relation to Time... In Relation to Others... Review

CH. 6 Choosing Your Destiny 77
Choosing the Hard Way over the Easy Way... The Disciplined Way Over the Undisciplined Way... The Thoughtful Way over the Thoughtless Way... Unity over Separation... People over Things... An Appropriately Centered Life-style... Review

CH. 7 Learning When To Be Quick And Slow 93
  Quick to Listen... Slow to Speak... Slow to Anger... Review

CH. 8 Healing Brokenness 105
  Reconciliation: Coming Together Again... Recognizing the Problem...
  Restoring the Relationship... Responding to Restoration...
  Renewal and Wholeness... Review

PART THREE - ON THE OTHER SIDE OF THE WALL

CH. 9 Excelling In Life Through Love 119
  Love Is Compassionate... Love Gives Comfort... Love Shares Concerns...
  Love Conquers All... Love Must Be Effectively Communicated... Review

CH. 10 Celebrating Life 129
  The Conditions for a Thankful Heart... The Blessings of a Thankful
  Heart... The Perils of an Unthankful Heart... The Thankful Heart Must
  Find Expression... The Thankful Heart Colors Our World... Review

CH. 11. Facing Life With Confidence 139
  Confidence: The Giant Slayer... Basic Confidence... Genuine Confidence...
  Ultimate Confidence... Why Ultimate Confidence Is Important...
  Achieving Confidence... Review

Conclusion 153

ACKNOWLEDGMENTS

To my son Chauncey Chapman Lever, who has provided me with tremendous insights into life and who has patiently awaited completion of this book.

To my son Charles Cauthen Lever, Jr., from whom I have learned so much and who painstakingly formatted the original manuscript.

To my parents Chauncey and Sara Lever, whose love and support have been a continual source of strength and encouragement throughout my life and in the writing of this book.

To my publisher, editor, and marketer — Burke Hedges, Steve Price, and Katherine Glover — who challenged and encouraged me to write this book and who have helped me see it through to fruition.

INTRODUCTION

⌐

BE A CLIMBER, NOT A QUITTER!

*Follow your bliss, and what look
like walls will turn into doors.*
— Joseph Campbell

Dr. Norman Vincent Peale, the philosopher/preacher
whose best-selling book *The Power of Positive Thinking* launched the
worldwide personal growth movement, loved to tell the story about
how he responded to the negative attitude of a wealthy friend named
George.

Dr. Peale was walking down the street one day when he saw George
approaching with an obvious scowl on his face.

"How are you, George?" Peale asked.

"Problems, problems," George answered with a frown. "I'm fed up with these problems. If you could get rid of all my problems, I'd gladly contribute $5,000 to your favorite charity."

"George," responded Peale, "I just might take you up on your offer. Why, only yesterday I was at a place where thousands of people reside and, to the best of my knowledge, not a single one of them has problems. Would you like to go there?"

George's face brightened at Dr. Peale's offer. "When can we leave?" he asked eagerly.

"I'll take you there tomorrow," Dr. Peale responded.

"Great!" George said. "Where are we going?"

"We're going to Woodlawn Cemetery," Dr. Peale responded with a straight face, "because the only people I know who don't have problems are dead."

If You Have a Pulse, You Have Problems

Dr. Peale's humorous anecdote drives home the point that everybody has problems in life. Too many of us seem to think that happy, successful people got that way because God smiled on them and gave them fewer problems than the rest of us.

Nothing could be further from the truth!

Contrary to popular opinion, those who experience higher levels of fulfillment in life are NOT those who experience lower levels of adversity. The truth is every human who ever lived has encountered walls of adversity in his or her life.

Some of the walls we encounter are so small that we can jump over them as easily as jumping over a mud puddle. But other walls are as tall and rugged as mountains. We couldn't climb straight up these walls if we tried, so if we want to move ahead in our lives, we have to find a way around them or through them.

Climbing the Walls

The premise of this book is that no matter how great the challenges in your life, you can find a way to move beyond them and grow from them. The key to overcoming challenges isn't giving in to them or ignoring them. *Quitting is NOT an option!* The key to living a happy, productive life is to view the walls in our lives as temporary obstacles, not permanent dead-ends.

Climbing walls is another way of saying you need to be persistent and determined if you are serious about accomplishing your goals in life. The great golfer Ben Hogan is an example of why it's important to climb walls.

In 1949, Hogan was recognized as one of the best golfers in the world. But on February 2, 1949, Hogan and his wife had a near-fatal head-on collision with a Greyhound bus. Hogan survived the crash, but he broke numerous bones on the left side of his body, including a crushed pelvis.

It took him 10 months to recover from the accident, and he had to teach himself to walk again. In fact, walking was so painful that after the accident, he limited his playing schedule to the major tournaments. Despite the walls of pain and inactivity that Hogan had to climb, he went on to play his best golf after the accident, culminating in 1953 when he won The Masters, the U.S. Open, and the British Open in the same year, a record that still stands today!

Ben Hogan's goal, you see, was to be the best golfer he could possibly be, and he was willing to climb every wall necessary to achieve that goal.

Building Doors

If *climbing walls* is about overcoming your problems through persistence, then *building doors* is about solving your problems through creativity and resourcefulness. You've probably heard of Grandma Moses, the great folk artist whose colorful paintings of rural life sell for hundreds of thousands of dollars today.

Amazingly, Grandma Moses didn't even start painting until she was 76 years old! Her main pastime before painting was needlework. But the arthritis in her hands made it too painful to continue the intricate needlework she loved, so she switched over to oil painting.

Grandma Moses, you see, was determined to lead a productive, creative life, which she did right up until her death at 101! When arthritis forced one door closed, she didn't give up — she just decided to build another door! She was determined to engage in a fulfilling, productive activity, and because she made the effort to build a door, she became a world-famous painter, even though she never had an art lesson in her life!

Like you and me, Ben Hogan and Grandma Moses had to find a way over, through, or around the walls in their lives. Life didn't hand them fame and fortune on a silver platter. They had to overcome huge adversities in order to get what they wanted.

Why I Wrote This Book

That's why I wrote this book — to make you aware of the fundamental universal principles that will empower you to climb the walls or build the doors in your life so that you, too, can realize your full potential.

Without a doubt you have walls in your life that are holding you back.

You may be struggling with your finances.

You may be fighting to hold your marriage together.

You may be enduring the loneliness and anger of a broken relationship.

You may be hurting from the betrayal of a friend or family member.

You may be suffering the estrangement of a child.

You may be grieving over the loss of a friend or loved one.

You may be fighting a disease.

You may be having run-ins with your boss.

You may be struggling to get a new business off the ground.

Because these walls of adversity won't go away on their own, *you have to be persistent* and keep trying until you climb those walls ... or *you have to be resourceful* and find a way to build a door through them.

The good news is that there are sound principles for dealing with adversity that enable us to turn stumbling blocks into stepping stones. *If You Can't Climb The Wall, Build A Door!* contains many time-tested principles that will enable you to overcome and move beyond the walls of adversity in your life, so that you can not only dream big dreams again, but you can also experience the joy and satisfaction of realizing those dreams.

Whatever the challenges in your life, I sincerely believe you can move beyond them and experience life more richly than ever before. It is my sincere hope and prayer that the proven principles discussed in this book will provide you with the wisdom and motivation to overcome the walls in your life ... and to become a more fulfilled, more complete person in the process.

Don't Just Try — TRIUMPH!

I'd like to close with an anonymous poem called *I Will Do More* that sums up the importance of standing tall in the face of adversity and making that second and third and fourth effort to climb the walls in our lives:

I Will Do More

I will do more than belong,
I will participate.

I will do more than care,
I will help.

I will do more than believe,
I will be kind.

I will do more than dream,
I will work.

I will do more than teach,
I will inspire.

I will do more than earn,
I will enrich.

I will do more than give,
I will serve.

I will do more than live,
I will grow.

I will do more than be friendly,
I will be a friend.

I will do more than be a citizen,
I will be a patriot.

With apologies to the author, I'd like to add one more stanza:

*I will do more than try,
I WILL TRIUMPH!*

My friend, you, too, can triumph! You don't have to remain boxed in by the walls in your life. You don't have to settle for living in the dark shadows of your personal walls.

You can feel the sun on your face ... you can make good things happen in bad times ... if only you'll CLIMB THE WALL OR BUILD A DOOR!

See you on the other side of the wall!

PART 1

~

Up Against the Wall

*Prosperity is a great teacher;
adversity is a greater.*
— William Hazlitt

CHAPTER 1

~

CONFRONTING LIFE'S CHALLENGES

If you have made mistakes, even serious mistakes,
there is always another chance for you. And sup-
posing you have tried and failed again and again,
you may have a fresh start any moment you choose,
for this thing that we call "failure" is not the falling
down, but the staying down.

— Mary Pickford

A number of years ago a newspaper photographer was called in by his editor to photograph a fire that was burning out of control in Palos Verdes, California.

The editor told the photographer he had to spring into action immediately if the story was to make the next edition. The photographer was instructed to go to the airport, where he would find a plane waiting, fly out to the fire and photograph it, and then return before the afternoon edition.

The photographer gathered together his equipment as quickly as possible and ran out of the building into the parking lot. He hopped into his car and sped to the airport. He drove to the end of a runway, where he found a plane revved up and ready to go, and he jumped on board.

When the plane rose to 5,000 feet, he began to remove his camera and other equipment from his bag. He instructed the pilot to fly as low as possible over the fire so that he could photograph it.

There was a brief moment of silence before the photographer heard this bone-chilling question from the cockpit:

"U-u-uh, you are the instructor, aren't you?"

Problems Find Us or We Find Them

One can only imagine the shock and the horror that both the photographer and pilot must have felt when they realized there had been a mix-up.

The photographer was looking for a seasoned pilot, and the student pilot was looking for a seasoned instructor. The photographer and pilot were both doing their best to do their jobs just right, and everything seemed to be going just fine, when all of a sudden trouble found its way into their lives.

Like the pilot and photographer, all too often we find ourselves in dire situations. Sometimes problems enter our lives unprovoked, and on other occasions, we create the problems in our lives (quite often, I might add, with the best of intentions). But no matter what the cause, the result is always the same. Problems will visit our lives, whether we like it or not.

Big Decisions Can Create Big Problems

The movie *Steel Magnolias* tells the story of a southern family consisting of a mother, a father, a daughter, and two sons. The daughter is a beautiful girl who is a diabetic. She falls in love with a young attorney but considers backing out of her upcoming marriage after a doctor tells her that she shouldn't bear children.

Although most diabetic women can have children, her diabetes was so severe that her body would be dangerously strained by a pregnancy. If she were to become pregnant, she could experience organ failure and death. She appears to resolve the matter and gets married. Much to the chagrin of her mother, however, the daughter announces that she's pregnant.

She gives birth to a beautiful baby boy, and in the process her kidneys fail. She is forced to receive dialysis treatment to live. In an effort to spare her daughter, the mother donates one of her kidneys for a transplant. Although the kidney transplant is a success, the daughter's body is never able to fully recover from the pregnancy, and she dies shortly after her child's first birthday.

In both stories, when the individuals were confronted with their life-and-death problems, they no doubt felt that their lives were out of control. In the case of the photographer, he stepped into a situation that he was unaware of. In the case of the daughter in *Steel Magnolias*, she created a problem for herself, even though she knew the consequences could turn out to be fatal. In both cases, the individuals involved must have been overwhelmed by the troubles that beset them.

Out of Control

From time to time, we all get ourselves into predicaments where our lives seem to be out of control. It is important to note, however, that it's not the challenges that determine our fate in life but the manner in which we choose to deal with those challenges that makes all the difference.

True, we can't always choose the challenges that we'll face in our lives. But we can choose our response. The one thing we all have in common is the fact that adversity, affliction, suffering — or whatever we may want to call it — is a part of life. That's a given. We can't choose NOT to face adversity. But we can choose the manner in which we deal with adversity, and those choices will ultimately determine who we are today and who we will become tomorrow.

Dr. Norman Vincent Peale was right when he noted that the only people who don't have problems are dead. If you don't believe it, all you have to do is to open up the newspaper and see how many problems are in the world today.

Stress: A Major Problem in Our Lives

In the United States we appear to have more than our fair share of problems, and it seems that more and more of these problems are related to the stress and strain of modern-day living.

For example, did you know that Americans will spend over a billion dollars in over-the-counter sleep aids this year? Experts estimate that one out of every three adults in this country has some form of sleeping disorder. And did you know that in the early '90s, the number one-selling prescription drug in America was Tagamet, an over-the-counter medicine for soothing ulcers? It's obvious that stress is fast becoming a major epidemic in this country.

Stress: The Problem That Won't Go Away

A recent article in my local newspaper, the *Tampa Tribune*, pointed out that stress "was once a good thing, designed to keep us alert and ready for action in times of danger. But what once kept us from becoming dinner is now eating us alive."

According to the author, John Ferri, stress was important to the survival of early humans because it allowed the body to bypass the use of energy for routine maintenance and repair of the body. It then diverted all the energy into a survival mode, either for flight from the enemy or to fight with the enemy. Ferri quips, "There's no reason to digest breakfast if you are about to become lunch."

The problem today is that stress has become chronic as opposed to acute and, therefore, the body may remain in the "stress-alert mode" of diverting its energy into survival over extended periods of time. This unnatural state of constant anxiety can contribute to accelerated aging, including premature onset of weight gain, diabetes, osteoporosis, loss of reproductive functions, slow wound healing, high blood pressure, heart disease, strokes, and perhaps even cancer.

The point is this: Stress is a major problem in our lives, and it's not going to go away. Unmanaged, the wall of stress can rob us of the abundant life by prematurely aging us and taking years off our lives. The bad news is we can't snap our fingers and wish stress out of our lives. But the good news is we can learn coping mechanisms that will enable us to climb the wall of stress by effectively managing it.

BUILDING A SOUND FOUNDATION

If problems are an unavoidable part of living, the question that needs to be answered is this: *How do we go about formulating the strategies that will enable us to cope with problems when they come our way?*

Before I answer that question, I'd like to tell you the parable of the Wise and Foolish Builders. It's a parable that shares a number of timeless, proven principles concerning how to best prepare ourselves to cope with adversity.

In the parable there are two builders. The wise builder built his house on rock. The rain fell, the floods came, and the winds blew and beat on the house, but it didn't fall because it had been founded on rock. The foolish man, however, built his house on sand. The rain fell, and the floods came, and the winds blew and beat against his house, and it fell.

The profound truths of this parable are better understood if you're aware of the historical background to the story, which originated in ancient Palestine. In those days it was quite common for large rivers in the Middle East to completely dry up during the summer. And, of course, the dry riverbeds were very enticing building sites for "foolish builders" because it was easy to dig the foundation in the soft sand. Their lack of knowledge or industry, however, would soon come back to haunt them.

The wise builders, on the other hand, understood the dangers of building too close to the riverbeds, so they would build their houses on higher land near the base of the mountains. This meant the "wise builders" would have to dig their footings in rock, which required long hours of back-breaking labor.

When the September rains came, the dry riverbeds became raging rivers that quickly swept away everything in their path. The houses built on sand were swept away in an instant, while the houses built on rock would last for years and years.

There are five universal principles that we can learn from the parable of the Wise and Foolish Builders. In the coming pages we will examine each of these principles in more depth to see what they can teach us about climbing walls and building doors in our lives.

PRINCIPLE 1: ADVERSITY COMES TO ALL

The first principle the parable teaches us is that adversity visits everyone. It's an eternal truth that the walls of adversity in life confront both the wise and the foolish, the learned and the unlearned, the rich and the poor, the young and the old, and those of every race, creed, and color.

As I said earlier, the issue isn't whether or not adversity will visit us, because, rest assured, it will. The issue is how we deal with those adversities. The greatest geniuses throughout history, for example, didn't flourish because their lives were problem free. They had problems, just like you and I have problems. But they triumphed because they refused to allow their problems to wall in their talents.

Great Talents Overcome Great Problems

One of the great masterpieces of classical music is Handel's *Messiah*. Individuals have marveled at its beauty for nearly 250 years. And yet Handel composed this masterpiece five years after he had suffered a life-threatening heart attack.

Pablo Picasso didn't have health problems, but early in his career he had serious money problems. When he was a young, unknown painter struggling to make ends meet, he was often forced to burn his own paintings in the fireplace in order to keep warm.

Mozart struggled to make ends meet early in his career, also. At one point he was so poor that he couldn't even afford to buy wood to heat the shabby little room where he lived. During the winter he wrapped his hands in woolen socks as he composed the music that would make him great. His early years of poverty weakened his immune system and made him especially susceptible to diseases, and as a result, he caught tuberculosis and died before his 36th birthday.

Each of these individuals confronted tremendous walls of adversity in their lives, but they found a way over or through those walls. As a result, they made major contributions to humanity.

If Life Gives You Lemons, Make Lemonade

We all have problems that we must confront. In fact, it has been humorously noted that there are so many problems in the world that if Moses were to come down from Mt. Sinai today, the two tablets he would be carrying with him would be aspirin!

The joke is funny, but it points out a serious issue — we have so many problems that sometimes we feel overwhelmed! That's why I emphasize that the key to overcoming the walls in our lives is to *focus on the manner in which we deal with our problems*, as opposed to focusing on the problems themselves.

Edgar Jackson is famous for his classic story *Message of the Maples*, which contains an enduring message for every human. The basis for the story came from Jackson's struggle to overcome a huge wall of adversity in his life.

Prior to writing the story, Jackson had a stroke and lost his speech. When he recovered, he moved to a farm in Corinth, Vermont, where he met a writer named Edward Zieglar. Zieglar had read many of Jackson's books, and as a writer himself, had gained great respect for Jackson.

Zieglar was experiencing a number of serious personal problems, and he went to Jackson for help. Jackson talked with Zieglar for a while, and then invited him out into his pasture. Jackson walked over to a three-acre pasture that was encircled by maple trees planted by the former owner. Jackson pointed to the trees and explained that the former owner had planted them so that he wouldn't have to set posts for a fence.

The owner waited until the trees were sturdy, and then he ran barbed wire from one tree to the next. Jackson walked from tree to tree with Zieglar, pointing out how different maples had responded to the barbed wire wrapped around their sensitive skin. Some trees had incorporated the wires into their trunks, and grew strong and upright despite the barbed wire. But some of the trees never adjusted to the intrusion of the barbed wire, and they grew twisted and deformed.

People Are Like Maples

Jackson noted that people are like those maples. Some people encounter problems, adjust to those problems by incorporating them into their lives, and then continue on, growing tall and triumphant in the process. Others allow their difficulties to twist, distort and ruin their lives. The difference between trees and people is that trees can't choose how they will grow. People can.

Ann Landers, the syndicated columnist, put it like this:

"If I were asked to give what I consider the single most useful bit of advice for all humanity, it would be this: Expect trouble as an inevitable part of life, and when it comes, hold your head high, look it squarely in the eye and say, 'I will be bigger than you. You cannot defeat me.' Then repeat to yourself the most comforting of all words, 'This, too, shall pass.' Maintaining self-respect in the face of a devastating experience is of prime importance."

The first lesson that we learn from the parable of the Wise and Foolish Builders is that the manner in which we deal with adversity in life is what enables us to enjoy the abundant life. Each time we deal with a problem in life in an effective fashion and learn from it, it can become the foundation for facing problems in the future.

Failing Your Way to Success

This doesn't mean that when we confront the walls of adversity the first time around, or even the next, or the next, that we will be able to climb over them or to build doors of opportunity to pass through them. Failure is not necessarily bad. As Abraham Lincoln observed, "My great concern is not whether you have failed, but whether you are content with failure."

After all, success is simply getting up one more time than you have fallen down. Ultimately, as we confront the challenges before us, we will succeed, even in the midst of our failures, for we can learn some of our best lessons from our failures. Henry Ford believed that "failure is the opportunity to begin again, more intelligently." Our concern in life shouldn't be about the possibility of failing but rather about the opportunities we miss when we don't try.

We've all failed many times! We all fell down when we first walked. We all nearly drowned when we first tried to swim. We all have fallen off the bike the first time out without training wheels. We have all mispronounced words that we were learning for the first time — and sometimes we still do.

Did you know that R. H. Macy failed seven times before his first department store became a success? Did you know that English novelist John Creasey received 753 rejection slips before he published the first of his 564 books? And did you know that baseball legend Babe Ruth struck out 1,330 times along the way to hitting 714 runs? The concern shouldn't be for failure. The concern should be for the opportunities missed when we don't try. Just as an athlete trains to improve his level of performance, the walls of adversity that we confront provide training for life.

PRINCIPLE 2: THE EASY PATH MAY NOT BE THE BEST PATH

The second principle of life that the parable of the Wise and Foolish Builders teaches us is that the easy path is often not the best path. The foolish builder was the one who sought to build a house by expending as little time and energy as possible. But, in the end, the house couldn't endure the storm and even his minimal efforts were wasted. It took the wise builder more time, more materials, and more labor, but when the storms had passed, the house still remained standing.

The great men and women of every age have known that it's never enough to simply get by. Their sights have always been on the goal and not simply on the expediency of the moment. William A. Ward gave as his "recipe for success: Study while others are sleeping, work while others are loafing, prepare while others are playing, and dream while others are wishing." Strong advice, indeed!

Thomas Edison remarked that work wasn't something that was measured in hours but in terms of reaching one's goals. As a result, he always kept on his desk a clock that had no hands. That was to remind him that time wasn't the most important issue — reaching the goal was the most important issue. As you might imagine, Edison spent endless hours in his laboratory. When Edison remarked that invention was "98 percent perspiration and only 2 percent inspiration," he was speaking from experience.

Excellence: The Spirit of America

The United States has become the most powerful nation on earth because of the commitment of its founding leaders, who wouldn't settle for just getting by.

At times we have lost our way, as was the case in the automobile industry in the 1980s when Detroit's flawed cars allowed Japanese car makers to steal a huge segment of the market. But Detroit returned to the American spirit of excellence by dramatically improving its cars, and by the late '90s, GM and Ford were reporting record profits.

Commitment to excellence is the glory of capitalism, and it won't allow us to settle for second best. As long as we devote our resources and ingenuity to research and development, we will remain world leaders, no matter what industry we choose to compete in. A case in point is the pharmaceutical industry, which the United States dominates by producing 95 percent of the new drugs and medicines in the world each year.

It's when we go the extra mile, when we keep trying to scale the wall no matter how hard the going, that we become the very best that we can be. Sadly enough, we can deny ourselves the opportunity to experience the abundant life when we seek to simply get by, as was the case with the foolish builder.

Taking the easy way out reminds me of the way sharks adapt themselves to their environment. The shark is a remarkable creature. It grows to the size of its surroundings. Sharks born and raised in aquariums will fully mature at six inches in length. But if you were to take the same species and toss it into the ocean, it would grow to six feet! Such is the case in our own lives. If we take the easy way out and play it safe, we will never grow to our fullest potential. If, on the other hand, we seek challenges and opportunities that force us out of our "aquariums" or comfort zones, we will grow to the size of our new environment.

PRINCIPLE 3: ANTICIPATING CONSEQUENCES

The third principle of life that the parable of the Wise and Foolish Builders teaches us is the importance of having a vision. The man who built his house on sand had a very limited vision. He didn't anticipate what would happen to the riverbed in six months. If his vision had extended to a year, or a lifetime, he never would have selected the riverbed for his building site. Likewise, those who lack foresight will find that their plans and dreams will become washed out like the house built in the sand.

See Yourself as an Eagle, Not a Chicken

The story is told of a farmer who captured a young eaglet and placed it with his chickens. As the eaglet grew up among the chickens, it adapted to their ways and their environment and became just another chicken.

One day a naturalist came by the farm, and, looking at the chickens, said, "That's not a chicken, that's an eagle."

"That's right," said the farmer, "but he's no longer really an eagle. He's really a chicken because he eats chicken feed and does everything chickens do. That eagle will never fly."

The naturalist wanted to test the farmer's theory, so he tossed the eagle into the air. Sure enough, the eagle didn't fly, and nothing the naturalist did could get the eagle to fly.

One day the naturalist took the eagle to the top of a tall mountain as the sun was rising. At the top of the mountain the eagle spied another eagle, a bird just like himself, gliding gracefully through the sky. The eagle then realized that he was different from the chickens and grasped hold of a vision that he, too, could fly.

The eagle immediately uttered a wild screech and launched himself from the man's outstretched arms. The eagle flew upward, higher and higher into the sky, until he disappeared in the distance.

While he had lived with chickens, he had been unable to fly. Once he captured the vision that he was an eagle and could fly, then he was able to soar. And so it is in life. Until we develop a vision for our own lives, we, too, are unable to reach for the heights and become all that we are capable of becoming.

See the World for What It Can Become

A vision enables us to see the world not for what it is — *but for what it can become!* A vision enables us to see our neighbor not for who our neighbor is — but for *who our neighbor can become.* A vision enables us to see ourselves not for who we are — but for *who we can become.* A vision enables us to soar like the eagle and to reach new heights. A vision enables us to transcend the walls of adversity in life and see what is waiting for us on the other side. A vision enables us to plan ways to climb over the walls of adversity and empowers us to build doors when we can't get over them.

The man or woman who has no vision is like the house built upon sand. When the waters of life come, that individual will be all washed out. But for the individual who has vision, the water can be held back, avoided, or overcome, and as a result, greater things will follow.

PRINCIPLE 4: USING THE MIND TO AVOID "MIND FIELDS"

The fourth principle that we learn from the Wise and Foolish Builders is the importance of listening. The wise builder had obviously sought the advice of those who had gone before and had listened to that advice. By seeking wisdom and listening to the voices of experience, the wise builder learned that many rivers dried up during the summer. But in September, when the rains returned, the dry beds were filled once again. And so he built his house elsewhere.

John Philip Sousa, the legendary American composer of patriotic songs, composed the great march *The Stars and Stripes Forever.* One evening Sousa was in his hotel room when he heard an organ grinder playing his march in a slow, dragging manner.

Sousa ran out of his room and dashed out into the street. "Stop! Stop!" he called to the lazy organ grinder. "I did not compose a funeral march!"

He snatched the organ out of the hands of the organ grinder and began turning the handle vigorously. The music rushed out in a spirited, snappy manner, as it was intended. The organ grinder bowed low and smiled knowingly at the great composer.

The next evening Sousa heard the organ being played at the appropriate tempo. Not surprisingly, a large group of people had gathered around the organ grinder and were applauding his performance, and his tip box was overflowing with coins and dollar bills. Sousa then noticed that the organ grinder had attached a large sign to the front of his organ.

It read,*"Pupil of John Philip Sousa."*

Putting Wisdom into Action

The organ grinder had the wisdom to listen and put into action what he had learned, for he knew that he had learned it from the master. His decision to listen paid huge dividends.

Likewise, the journey through life is safest when we learn to listen to those who speak with authority. A soldier once said, "The best way to make it through a mine field is to follow someone who has already made it." Life is like a mine field with its many challenges and opportunities, and the journey is made much safer when we seek wise counsel along the way.

PRINCIPLE 5: ACTING AS A DREAM MAKER, NOT A DREAM TAKER

The fifth and final principle we learn from the parable is that it makes little difference what our vision is for life or how well we have listened if we don't act. The wise builder acted according to what he had heard and envisioned. As a result, he built his house upon rock.

We've all heard the old expression, "Action speaks louder than words." When it comes to climbing the walls in your life, action is everything. People who take action solve the problems in their lives. People who don't take action are destined to fritter their lives away.

Cafeteria America

There's a great story about an immigrant to America that illustrates the power of taking action. Years ago an ambitious young man immigrated to America from Europe. After being processed on Ellis Island, he went to a local cafeteria to get something to eat.

The immigrant took a seat and waited for someone to serve him.

No one did. Finally, a kind stranger stopped to tell the new immigrant how things worked in a cafeteria.

"Start at the end of the line," the stranger said. "Then get yourself a tray and select what you want as you go down the line. When you come to the other end of the line, they will tell you how much to pay for it."

Years later the immigrant told his grandson the story of eating in a cafeteria his first day in America, concluding his story with these words of wisdom:

"Life is a cafeteria in America. You can get anything you want if you are willing to pay the price. You can even have success itself. But you won't get it if you expect someone to bring it to you. You have to get up and get it for yourself."

When you think about it, that's really what action is all about — getting up and getting it yourself. When an interviewer asked Estée Lauder, the founder of one of the largest cosmetics companies in the world, her secret to success, she replied: "I can tell you one thing. I didn't get there by just wishing for it or dreaming about it or hoping for it. I got there by working for it." She understood the power of action, and she has reaped the benefits by becoming a multi-millionaire!

Being Ready Is Not Enough

Knofel Stanton, in his book *Check Your Commitment*, tells about an unforgettable experience he had while serving as a control tower supervisor in Japan. Two jet fighters were flying in formation and had started their landing descent when the lead pilot radioed, "I've just lost my wing man." This meant that one of the planes had gone down.

The control tower sprang into action by picking up the emergency phone and calling the rescue helicopter team that was on standby. Within 120 seconds of the phone being picked up, a rescue helicopter would be in the air.

The pilot descended below the clouds to see if he could find his wingman, who had bailed out and was floating in the ocean. The pilot circled his wingman for 20 minutes, continually reporting back the condition of his downed colleague. Each time the lead pilot radioed the control tower, he would earnestly inquire as to the location of the rescue helicopter. Though the procedure called for a rescue helicopter to be dispatched within two minutes of a report, the helicopter never arrived. Tragically, the wingman drowned.

15

Where was the rescue helicopter? It never got to the scene. At the investigation and hearing, it was discovered that the rescue team had decided to do some Christmas shopping at a military base 50 miles away.

The story is all the more tragic because the rescue team had the training and equipment that were required to save a life. But because they failed to take action in a timely manner, their preparation was useless. The moral is that if we don't act when the occasion calls for it, the consequences can be disastrous or even fatal.

Act Now, Not Later

Just before the Great Depression, a man named J. G. Roscoe envisioned building the tallest skyscraper in New York City. Some of his critics said that such a building was architecturally impossible. Others said that such a venture would be a financial disaster.

Nonetheless, J. G. Roscoe was determined to see his vision become a reality. In the fall of 1929, just before the great crash, Roscoe cashed out all of his stock so that he could invest the money in his project. He also persuaded many other investors to sell their stocks as well. Within months the stock market crashed, leaving literally millions of people impoverished.

A year later, with the support of the investors who had followed his advice, Roscoe began building his monumental skyscraper. Today Roscoe's dream, which he named the Empire State Building, still remains one of the biggest tourist attractions in New York City. How different things could have been had he not acted quickly and urged others to do the same.

Yes, the wise builder was wise because he acted. Not only was he able to see his vision become a reality, but, in so doing, he was able to experience fulfillment and satisfaction. In a very real way, our actions determine where our hearts lie.

Like the men and women in the stories I've just told you, the first step to climbing the walls of your life is to confront life's challenges. Only by confronting those challenges are we able to rise above them.

In the next chapter, titled "Living Above Adversity," you'll learn more about the principles that will empower you not only to face adversity in your life, but also to turn the stumbling blocks of adversity into stepping stones.

REVIEW

The secret to taking control of our lives — so that they don't take control of us — is to build an appropriate foundation. The parable of the Wise and Foolish Builders reminds us of five important principles.

Principle 1: Adversity comes to all

Everyone confronts walls of adversity. The question is whether or not these walls of adversity will become stumbling blocks or stepping stones. The answer depends on how we decide to confront these walls of adversity. If we seek to withdraw from them, they become stumbling blocks. If we seek to climb over them (or when that doesn't work, to build a door through them), then they can become stepping stones to the future.

Principle 2: The easy path may not be the best path

When we're willing to make the extra effort, to go the second mile, then this helps to ensure that the job will get done, that it will get done properly, and when it's done, that it will last.

Principle 3: Anticipating consequences

Vision enables transformation to occur in life. As a result, we're able to transcend the way things are in order that we might see them as they can become.

Principle 4: Using the mind to avoid "mind fields"

Listening enables us to avoid the "mine fields of life" by learning from the experience and knowledge of others.

Principle 5: Acting as a dream maker, not a dream taker

Action enables dreams to become reality and enables us to overcome the walls of adversity. You are either a part of the solution or a part of the problem. That makes you either a dream maker or a dream taker. The choice is yours and yours alone.

CHAPTER 2

~

LIVING ABOVE ADVERSITY

Adversity causes some men to break —
others to break records.
> — William A. Ward

Several years ago the president of the Pontiac Division of GM received this perplexing complaint letter:

I know this is the second time that I have written you, and I am not surprised that I have not heard a response from you. However, it is a fact that my family has a tradition of eating ice cream every night after dinner. Since we do not eat the same flavor each night, we allow the family to vote after dinner and then I go down to the ice cream store to pick it up. Furthermore, it is a fact that whenever I go and pick up vanilla ice cream, my car will never start when I come out of the store. However, when I pick up any flavor other than vanilla, my car will start. Why is it that vanilla ice cream keeps my car from starting?

The president of Pontiac was understandably skeptical of the letter, but he sent an engineer to check out the story. The engineer, having no experience in relating vanilla ice cream to mechanical problems, had no idea what to expect. Nevertheless, he called the man and made arrangements to have dinner with the family the following night.

On the night they had dinner, the family voted for vanilla, the engineer and the man drove down to the ice cream store, they purchased vanilla ice cream, and when they returned to the car, sure enough, it wouldn't start!

The second night the family chose chocolate ice cream, and true to form, the car started as soon as the two men left the ice cream store. The third night they chose strawberry ice cream, and the car started again. The fourth night they chose vanilla, and, as always, the car failed to start when the men left the store.

The engineer was a rational person, and he began taking meticulous notes of everything that went on, from the type of gas purchased to the weather. After a few days he discovered an apparent link. The engineer observed that the man spent more time in the ice cream store when he purchased flavors other than vanilla. The reason was simple: Vanilla was the most popular flavor, and the ice cream store manager provided a separate box for vanilla. Consequently, the customers who ordered vanilla could move in and out of the store more quickly than customers who ordered less popular flavors.

Cause and Effect Not Always Obvious

Upon further investigation, the engineer discovered that the problem with the car was a vapor lock that would dissipate in a few minutes. The man spent more time in the store when he ordered any flavor other than vanilla, which allowed the vapor lock enough time to dissipate. When he purchased vanilla, however, he got back into the car before the vapor lock had time to dissipate, resulting in a car that wouldn't start. The mechanical problem of the car was due to a vapor lock and not the flavor of the ice cream.

Interestingly enough, our assessments of life can be just as misdirected and misguided as the man who thought buying vanilla ice cream caused his car to malfunction. If we are careless and hasty in analyzing the problems in our life, then we're more likely to treat the SYMPTOMS as if they were the walls, rather than treating the CAUSE, which is the real wall.

Treating the Symptom Is the Easy Way Out

A perfect example of treating the symptoms instead of the cause is our national dependence on sleeping pills and "nerve pills," like Valium. These drugs do a great job of treating the SYMPTOMS by making the user feel better temporarily, but unless the real CAUSE of the problem is treated, it will never go away. Treating symptoms is the easy way out, and we learned from the foolish builder that taking the easy way out is a prescription for disaster!

Dr. Scott Peck, author of the best-seller *The Road Less Traveled*, argues that pain is necessary in life, for without coping with pain, there is no growth. He goes so far as to observe that the root cause of every psychological problem is the individual's mental effort to avoid pain. Peck understands that avoiding pain is not the answer to living an abundant life.

The key to life is learning to cope with your problems and growing from them, as opposed to avoiding them. In other words, healthy, fulfilled people find productive ways to negotiate the walls of adversity, rather than taking a pill that makes them temporarily forget about the walls in their lives.

The Bible Is the Story of Struggle

The Bible is the story of the struggle of humanity throughout history. We see Moses struggle when he is unable to enter into the promised land; We see Hannah struggle because she is unable to bear children; We see Mary and Martha struggle over their brother's death; and we see Jesus struggle in the wilderness, in the Garden of Gethsemane, and finally, on the cross.

A lot has changed since the days of the Bible, but human struggles will always be with us, no matter how much "progress" we make. We see suffering in the world today in terms of unemployment, divorce, illiteracy, estrangement, war, hunger, homelessness, disease, illness, death — the list goes on and on. All around us we see and hear of the suffering of others, and we experience it in our own lives in physical, emotional, and spiritual dimensions.

Adversity Is a Blessing in Disguise

Adversity and suffering, though always a challenge and often quite painful, don't have to defeat us. The old saying, "It's not whether you win or lose, but how you play the game" contains great truth. If we try to escape from adversity, then we step backward in life and learn nothing. On the other hand, when we confront adversity head on — whether we defeat it or suffer a temporary defeat — we can learn and grow from the experience.

Although we would rather travel through life without experiencing adversity, it does in a very real way shape us into the individuals that we become. And, quite often, the manner in which adversity shapes us can be good for us if we learn to live above it, as opposed to underneath it.

How is it that adversity can actually move us ahead in life and not hold us back? There are six proven principles that we can learn from confronting adversity. They are as follows:

1) Adversity changes our perceptions

2) Adversity brings out the best in us

3) Adversity makes us stronger

4) Adversity opens up new opportunities

5) Adversity compels us to change

6) Adversity builds confidence

Let's take a look at each of these principles in more detail and examine how they can help us climb the walls and build the doors in our lives.

PRINCIPLE 1: ADVERSITY CHANGES OUR PERCEPTIONS

All too often we spend too much time and energy worrying about the little things in life and fail to recognize the larger blessings and opportunities that lie before us. Some of the best advice I can give to people is "don't major in the minor things." And let's face it, when it's all said and done, most things we fret about in life are minor things!

I'd like to tell you a story that will explain what I mean when I say that adversity changes our perceptions. The story concerns

Dr. Paul W. Brand, a world-renowned expert in leprosy who was chief of the rehabilitation branch of the Leprosarium in Carville, Louisiana. Dr. Brand had an experience one evening that would change his perceptions — literally overnight!

Dr. Brand had just arrived from an exhausting transatlantic flight and had taken off his shoes to get ready for bed. Suddenly, he noticed that one of his heels was numb. The numbness in his heel terrified him. He knew that numbness in a patch of skin was the telltale sign of leprosy.

Dr. Brand was renowned for his restorative surgery on lepers in India. He had persuaded himself and his staff that leprosy was no longer contagious after it reached a certain stage. But privately he had always questioned whether he could contract the dreaded disease even after the noncontagious stage had been reached.

He rose from his bed, almost mechanically, to get a sharp pin. He stuck the pin into his numb heel and felt nothing. He drove the pin deeper into his heel, until a speck of blood appeared, but still he felt nothing.

All through the night he thought about what it would mean if he had contracted leprosy. He knew such a diagnosis would shatter the confidence of his staff and threaten his ministry to lepers. And, of course, he would have to isolate himself from his family so that they would not contract the dreaded disease.

Thank God for Pain

In the morning he got up again to confirm the results of the night before. He pricked his heel with the sharp pin ... and let out a yell! How blessed was the sensation of pain! It was a sign that he was alive, and that he had not contracted leprosy. From that day forward, whenever Brand turned an ankle, cut a finger, or experienced pain, he would cry out, *"Thank God for pain!"*

Pain is not something that we usually think of giving thanks for. Dr. Brand, however, came to experience pain not as something bad that signals a problem, but as something good that is representative of health and wholeness. Additionally, he gained a new appreciation for his own well-being and health. As we experience adversity, we learn to put things in their proper perspective. When we are faced with the bigger problems of life, then the little concerns, like getting stuck in an elevator or lost in traffic, don't seem to be nearly so important.

PRINCIPLE 2: ADVERSITY BRINGS OUT THE BEST IN US

The saying, "All sunshine makes a desert" reminds us of the importance of adversity. Where there is no adversity, we become complacent with who we are and lose the drive to advance ourselves. As a result, we turn ourselves into emotional and creative deserts.

There's an old saying in Florida that the ponds populated by alligators have the healthiest fish. Why? Because the fish have to stay alert or the alligators will have them for lunch. In the same way, adversity is an emotional alligator that keeps people strong and alert — and alive!

New Zealand is a paradise for many birds because there are no natural predators there and food is plentiful. But there is a downside to this bird paradise. Because the birds don't need to flee from predators and food is so easy to come by, many of the native birds lost their ability to fly!

In fact, New Zealand is the home to more flightless birds — the kiwi and the penguin are prime examples — than any other country in the world. Ironically, scientists believe these flightless birds once had wings, but they have since lost them from neglect.

Learning from Our National Symbol

We can see more proof of the value of adversity by examining the way mother eagles encourage their young to become independent. The female eagle, you see, builds her nest in only the highest trees or the loftiest mountain ledges.

First she builds the foundation of her nest with hard, sharp objects, like thorns and jagged stones. Then she makes the nest warm and comfortable for her baby eaglets by lining it with soft materials, like wool, feathers, and fur from animals she has killed.

As the eaglets grow older and the time comes for them to seek their independence and find food on their own, the mother eagle stirs up the nest with her sharp talons. In so doing, the sharp protrusions beneath the lining of the nest are exposed, stabbing the young eaglets.

Eventually, the youngsters become so miserable that they leave the nest to seek a more comfortable home. The mother eagle isn't being cruel to her young ones. She is merely doing what is best for them if they are to survive on their own. Without adversity, the eaglets would never be forced to mature and realize their full, majestic potential.

The same is true of humans. Without adversity we would never feel compelled to reach our fullest potential. Scholars note that some of the greatest technological advances have taken place in the colder climates of the world because the inhabitants were forced to struggle against the elements and nature. It is, therefore, quite true that necessity is the mother of invention and that adversity builds character.

This is true in life and in faith. It is, more often than not, when we become dissatisfied with the way things are that we begin to find new ways of growing and becoming the individuals that we can become. Depending on how we choose to respond to adversity, it can either cause us to withdraw or compel us to move ahead.

When Second Place Isn't Good Enough

Bob Mathias, for example, was the gold medalist in the decathlon in the 1952 Olympic games. In that same year, Milt Campbell was the silver medalist in the decathlon. At the next Olympic games in 1956, Campbell became the gold medalist in the decathlon and Rafer Johnson had to settle for the silver medal. Sure enough, in the 1962 Olympics, Rafer Johnson won the gold medal in the decathlon while C. K. Yang settled for the silver. Can you guess who won at the 1966 Olympics? That's right, C. K. Yang became the gold medalist in '66, setting a new record in the decathlon in the process!

The lesson is unmistakable: Quite often in life we find that it's not until we're unhappy with the way things are that we become the very best that we can become. The walls of adversity that confront us in life compel us to grow and develop and mature in life.

PRINCIPLE 3: ADVERSITY MAKES US STRONGER

Many individuals remain on the sidelines of life until they feel that they are needed, and then they spring into action. That is the way heroes are born. A need arises and someone rises to the occasion, driven by compassion, courage, or righteous indignation, and lives are changed forever.

A German legend tells the story of an eccentric baron who lived in a castle on a cliff overlooking the Rhine. His great desire was to create the biggest Aeolian harp the world had ever seen. (Aeolian harps get their name from the Greek god of the wind, Aeolus, and they produce sound only when the wind passes over their strings).

The baron decided to create his giant harp by stretching wires from one tower of his castle to another, reasoning that the wind would blow across the strings, creating beautiful music. The soft breezes blew throughout the castle, but there was no music. Then one evening a dreadful tempest struck the area, and the mighty winds set the wires to music. The delighted baron could hear the sounds of his giant Aeolian harp even above the clamor of the tempest.

The point is that gentle breezes weren't enough to make the harp spring into action. It took the magnitude of a tempest to sound the music of the giant Aeolian harp. How often have we known others, and even ourselves, to be silent in the calm days of prosperity, only to find in the midst of a tempest the power and strength of our own music?

Handel's "Messiah"

The great musician Frederich Handel threatened to give up on life during a period of severe suffering and adversity. The right side of his body had become paralyzed, all of his funds had been used up, and his creditors were threatening him with imprisonment if he didn't pay his bills. This was Handel's darkest hour, and he considered taking the easy way out by taking his life.

But, at that lowest point in his life, Handel decided to climb the wall instead of giving in to it. It was during this time of personal torment that Handel wrote one of the greatest masterpieces in the history of music, *The Messiah*. This story reminds us that great strength often comes in the moments in which we perceive ourselves to be weakest.

Making Beautiful Music

Once again, all we have to do is observe nature to confirm that, more often than not, adversity is an ally, not an enemy. Did you know that the sound of the violin is determined by both the type of wood used in its construction and the skill and training of the violinist? Interestingly enough, it's not the type of tree that is of primary importance to creating a world-class violin so much as the adversity that the tree has had to endure.

That's why today some of the choicest wood for making violins comes from the timberline of the Rockies, 12,000 feet above sea level. It is there, where the winds blow so fiercely that the bark cannot grow on the windward side and the branches can only grow in one direction, that some of the world's most resonant wood for violins is to be found. The same trees, in a less challenging environment, would produce only mediocre instruments.

This principle is true for people as it is for trees: Just as the rigors of training make the musician, the athlete, the soldier, and the musician stronger, so, too, can the walls of adversity make each of us stronger.

PRINCIPLE 4: ADVERSITY OPENS UP NEW OPPORTUNITIES

When adversity strikes, we often want to withdraw into our own world of self-pity. Interestingly enough, however, quite often the very adversity we're seeking to avoid is the same adversity that creates new opportunities in our life.

The young Hungarian artist Arpad Sebesy was once commissioned to paint a portrait of Elmer Kelen, a multi-millionaire. Sebesy spent weeks on the portrait. The task was especially difficult because Kelen agreed to set aside only three short sessions to pose for the artist. As a result, Sebesy was forced to complete most of the portrait from memory.

Despite the limitations, Sebesy thought the portrait was a pretty good likeness of Kelen. Unfortunately, Kelen did not think so. The arrogant millionaire said that it was a rotten likeness of him, and he refused to pay for the portrait. The young painter had spent hours and hours working diligently on the painting, and suddenly he realized that he would have nothing to show for it.

As the millionaire was leaving the studio, the artist inquired, "Would you sign a letter saying you have refused the portrait because it didn't resemble you?"

Portrait of a Thief

Kelen agreed, feeling relieved that he could get off so easily. Months later, when the Society of Hungarian Artists opened its exhibition in the Gallery of Fine Arts in Budapest, Kelen's phone began to ring. Soon he appeared in the gallery to find the portrait that Sebesy had painted of him to be on display with the title, *Portrait of a Thief.*

The arrogant millionaire demanded that the painting be taken down. When the manager refused, Kelen threatened to sue because the painting would make him the laughingstock of the community. The manager then pulled out the letter Kelen had signed stating that he'd refused the painting because it didn't resemble him.

The millionaire realized he had no recourse but to buy the painting. The young artist not only had the last laugh, he also turned his adversity into a handsome profit, for when the millionaire sought to buy his portrait, he was astonished to learn that the price was now 10 times higher than the original!

You see, the struggling artist had refused to give in to adversity. Instead, he thought of a way to build a door by being resourceful and creative instead of giving in to bitterness and anger. In short, the artist discovered a valuable principle: New opportunities often visit us in times of adversity, for when one door closes, another opens.

Tragedies Often Turn into Triumphs

It's one of life's greatest ironies that incidents that we think of as tragic often turn out to be the best things that ever happened to us. The following story of a shipwrecked sailor is a vivid example of bad experiences that turn out for the best.

It seems that the sole survivor of a shipwreck found himself stranded on an uninhabited island. With a superhuman effort, the sailor was able to build a very crude hut. He placed everything he could salvage from the wreck into the hut, and then spent his days scanning the horizon for a rescue ship.

Saved by Misfortune

Three years passed by and not a single ship appeared on the horizon. One day, when the sailor returned home from hunting, he found that his hut had caught fire and burned completely to the ground. He was crushed by this unfortunate turn of events, for now he had absolutely nothing except the clothes on his back. This had to be the worst day of his life.

Several hours later, however, a ship arrived to rescue him. The captain told the elated sailor, *"You're a lucky man. We would have passed right by your island if we hadn't seen the smoke from the fire you set."*

What the sailor perceived as his biggest setback early in the day turned out to be his greatest blessing later in the day. If we take time to think about it, I think you'd agree that all of us have experienced episodes in our lives where a perceived tragedy turned into a major blessing.

That's why we should never give up trying to climb the walls in our lives. If the sailor had given in to his despair and hanged himself from the nearest tree, he'd never have lived to experience the joy of being rescued, proving once again that quitting is NOT an option!

PRINCIPLE 5: ADVERSITY COMPELS US TO CHANGE

The sailor's story reminds me of a real-life story of someone whose life was altered for the better because he had to face a personal tragedy. You probably recognize the name of the person I'm going to tell you about because he's a singer who has sold more records than any recording artist in history — Julio Iglesias.

Prior to becoming a singer, Iglesias was a professional soccer player. But his soccer career came to an abrupt end when he was involved in a serious car crash in Madrid. Iglesias remained bed-ridden for a year and a half after the accident, and a sympathetic nurse brought Iglesias a guitar to help him pass the time during his long recovery.

Although Iglesias had never had any musical aspirations prior to his accident, his adversity forced him to open the door that led to his wildly successful musical career. Iglesias seized his new opportunity and turned his tragedy into one of the greatest triumphs in the history of popular music.

Like Julio Iglesias, we, too, need to learn to look for the opportunities that become available to us when other opportunities are lost, and we need to be willing to change the course of our lives when adversity pushes us in a new direction.

Turning Disadvantages into Advantages

Have you heard the old saying, "The only constant is change"? The saying has been around since the early Greeks, so obviously it contains ageless wisdom. For sure, we initiate many of the changes we make in our lives. But adversity provokes many of our major life changes, and more often than not those changes improve us.

Joe Montana, the Hall of Fame-bound quarterback of the San Francisco 49ers, is a case in point. The master of the short pass, Montana was arguably the finest quarterback in the history of the NFL.

In fact, Montana threw long passes so rarely that many "experts" questioned whether or not he had a sore arm that prevented him from throwing long. Before one Super Bowl, sportscaster John Madden challenged Montana's throwing ability, asking, "Joe, are you going to start throwing deep this game?"

"No," Montana responded.

"Why not? pressed Madden. "Do you have a sore arm?"

"No, my arm's not sore," Montana replied. "I can throw a long pass. But we don't have any plays to throw deep, so we never practice throwing deep."

Madden looked dumbfounded. "I don't get it. Why don't you have any plays to throw deep?" Montana smiled before delivering his surprising answer.

When Less Is More

"Most teams have a hundred-yard artificial turf field and a hundred-yard grass field to practice on," he explained. "We don't. We have only one field that is half artificial turf and half grass. When the rains come in December, the players have to wear either artificial turf shoes or cleats, depending on which half of the field we are practicing on.

"The players don't like playing with cleats on artificial turf or with artificial turf shoes on grass. So, when we practice, we put the ball on the 20-yard line, which means we have about 30 yards to work with. You can't throw very deep with only 30 yards, and even the pregame warm-up limits you to half a field. So, that's why I don't throw deep."

You see, Joe Montana was a great quarterback because he turned a disadvantage into an advantage by changing his approach to the game. Others might have used his situation to complain or make excuses for failure. But Montana realized that even in the midst of adversity, there are opportunities to grow and develop.

In the words of Robert Schuller, Joe Montana turned "a scar into a star" when he used an inferior field to develop the short pass. When we adapt to adversity instead of allowing it to break us, we often find that it motivates us to venture out beyond our comfort zones and to avail ourselves of opportunities that we never noticed before.

PRINCIPLE 6: ADVERSITY BUILDS CONFIDENCE

Every time we pass through a difficult experience in life, we gain confidence in our ability to go through it again. Furthermore, we become less fearful of the adversities that may lie before us, and in turn, we're able to take the risks necessary to grow and mature.

I recall the time my first son began to walk. I wanted to hold his hands so he wouldn't fall. Eventually I learned to let go of his hands, but I would always run to catch him before he fell.

Finally, my wife said, "If you will let him walk on his own, he'll learn not to fall, and you won't have to catch him anymore." Sure enough, in a couple of days he was doing just fine on his own. As he learned to get up and maintain his balance on his own, he soon conquered his falling.

This simple anecdote confirms a profound principle: If, on the one hand, we seek to withdraw from adversity, we will lack confidence and fail to grow and mature. On the other hand, when we confront adversity head on, we gain confidence and succeed in moving ahead in life.

A Story for the Ages

The famous English writer Somerset Maugham wrote a story about a janitor at St. Peter's Church in London. The janitor was illiterate, and the young vicar became concerned that the janitor's inability to read and write would interfere with his job, so he fired the janitor.

Unemployed and with limited skills, the janitor — in a true entrepreneurial spirit — opened a small tobacco stand. The stand grew into a store, the store prospered, and, in time, the venture evolved into a very profitable chain of stores worth millions.

One day a smug banker challenged the illiterate man with a mean-spirited question: "You've done well for someone who is illiterate, but where would you be if you could read and write?"

The illiterate man thought for a moment before replying, "Well, I reckon I'd still be a janitor at St. Peter's Church in Neville Square."

Stepping up to Life's Challenges

The former janitor could have allowed his unemployment to destroy his self-esteem, but instead it drove him to step up to life's challenges and try something else. In the process, he gained a renewed sense of confidence in who he was and what he was about.

Genuine confidence comes from within as the result of who we REALLY are, and what we are REALLY about, and not as the consequence of external credentials. Remember, "Professionals built the *Titanic*, amateurs built the ark."

REVIEW

Adversity and suffering, though always challenges, don't have to defeat us. In fact, when we learn to live above adversity — as opposed to beneath it — we can work it to our advantage.

Living above adversity simply means that we're willing to face it head on and to learn from it, as opposed to withdrawing from it and allowing it to hold us down and back. There are six fundamental principles that enable us to move forward in the face of adversity:

Principle 1: Adversity changes our perceptions

Principle 2: Adversity brings out the best in us

Principle 3: Adversity makes us stronger

Principle 4: Adversity opens up new opportunities

Principle 5: Adversity compels us to change

Principle 6: Adversity builds confidence

Parting Anecdote

Rising Above Adversity

World-renowned architect, Frank Lloyd Wright, was once awakened in the middle of the night by a phone call from a frantic client whose roof was leaking so badly that his living room was flooded.

"What should I do?," the caller inquired of the great architect.

Wright responded calmly, *"Rise above it!"* Then he hung up the phone.

This humorous anecdote points out a sober truth: Adversity and suffering are inevitable in life, but they're also essential to our growth and development. When we rise above adversity, we learn from it, and if we don't allow it to break us, we'll find new opportunities to enrich our lives and to become all that we've been created to become.

CHAPTER 3

～

MOVING BEYOND A ROCK AND A HARD PLACE

*Sometimes you have to leave the city of your comfort
and go into the wilderness of your intuition. You
can't get there by bus, only by hard work and risk
and by not quite knowing what you're doing. But
what you'll discover will be wonderful. What you'll
discover will be yourself.*

— Hawkeye Pierce
Doctor in the movie M*A*S*H

In the days of the California Gold Rush, an old miner
went into town to cash in his gold. When he arrived in town, he tied
up his old mule in front of the saloon and began walking down to the
surveyor's office.

A cowboy looking for trouble came out of the saloon and shouted,
"Hey, old timer, do you know how to dance?"

"No, sonny, I never learned how to," the old timer replied.

"Well, you'd better learn," the cowboy said, and he pulled out his
pistol and began shooting at the old timer's feet. The old timer began

to jump up and down and, before long, he was dancing pretty well. But what the cowboy didn't realize was that as he was shooting, the old timer was counting the number of bullets he had left in his pistol.

When the old timer knew that the cowboy had fired his last bullet, he pulled out a shotgun from the saddle on his mule. He stuck the gun barrel under the cowboy's chin, and asked, "Sonny, have you ever kissed a mule?"

The cowboy said quietly, *"No, sir. But I sure would like the opportunity."*

Regaining Control of Our Lives

How often in life do we feel as though we've lost control in our lives because — like the old timer and the cowboy — we feel caught between a rock and a hard place? How often do we feel like the characters in the story, spending precious time dancing to other people's music and kissing other people's mules?

It doesn't have to be like that!

We don't have to remain stuck in the middle with nowhere to go. We do have a choice in how we respond to our circumstances, no matter how difficult those circumstances might be.

The Story of the Four Lepers

The book of II Kings tells a remarkable story that serves as a perfect illustration of what it means to be caught between a rock and a hard place.

The king of Syria assembles his entire army and lays siege to the city of Samaria. The siege lasts for so long that it practically reduces the city to starvation.

At the same time, four lepers are starving just outside the gates of the city, and they discuss their options for survival. They don't want to go back into the city, for they'll surely starve there. They don't want to remain where they are, for they'll surely die when the Syrians attack the gates.

The lepers figure that doing something is better than doing nothing, for to remain where they are will be certain death. So they decide to go forward to the Syrian camp and surrender. When they arrive in the Syrian camp, they're surprised to discover that the Syrians have fled. It seems the Syrians had heard a great noise and thought their enemies were attacking them, so they fled into the hills without bothering to break camp.

Entering the empty camp, the lepers are amazed to find plenty of fresh food and supplies, and they eat until they're full. They gather up the spoils from the empty tents and then return to the city to share the good news.

This ancient story is an important one because it offers valuable insights into what we should do when we find ourselves caught between a rock and a hard place. In the following pages we will discuss the three proven principles that the story of the lepers teaches, principles that will empower you to move beyond a rock and a hard place in your life. The three principles are as follows:

1) Avoid the pitfalls of the past

2) Conquer your complacency

3) Acquiesce to abundance

PRINCIPLE 1: AVOID THE PITFALLS OF THE PAST

First of all, the story of the four lepers reminds us that we can't go back. How often do we seek to live in the past? Perhaps you long for the way things once were. Or perhaps you feel that the unpleasantness of your past has locked you into a never-ending cycle of failure. In short, you feel trapped by your past.

When World War I came, President Woodrow Wilson said, "We shall be neutral in name and in fact." But that's not the way life is. When the whole world around you is at war, you can't be neutral and at peace. We learned that lesson quickly during WW I. Likewise, we can't be neutral about our past. We have to let it go, whether we want to or not.

Learning a Lesson in Life

I recall playing the board games Parcheesi and Candyland with my son Chapman when he was seven years old. Parcheesi is a game in which you move the pieces forward by rolling the dice. Candyland is a game in which you move the pieces of the game by picking up a card.

I noticed that as we played the games, as soon as Chapman discovered he was behind, he would want to start over again. He wanted to go back and begin anew. I used the game as an opportunity to help Chapman learn an important lesson in life — namely, that you can't always start over. You can't always go back. You must move ahead.

As we played the games over and over, he gradually learned that just because I was ahead didn't mean that I was going to win. The most important lesson he learned was that in order to win you always have to keep moving ahead. You can't go back!

In a similar manner, we can't live in the past. Sometimes we can become imprisoned in the past, and when we do, we're unable to live in the present or move forward into the future.

Unbending the Twig

The old expression "As the twig is bent, so grows the tree" sums up the impact that our childhood has on us when we become adults. But let's face it, not everyone grows up in an ideal family setting, and as a result, many people suffer the wounds of their childhood long after they've left home.

It's easy to blame our less-than-perfect childhoods on our failings as adults and to accept the negative image that has been stamped on us from infancy. But if we're to enjoy a truly abundant life, we have to let go of our past and move beyond a rock and a hard place.

Amazing Story of Bill Wilson

I'd like to tell you a remarkable story of Bill Wilson, a man who triumphed over the pitfalls of his past. One morning when Bill was only six years old, his mother took him downtown. Just as she was about to enter a store, she instructed Bill to sit on the curb and wait until she returned.

"Honey, just wait for me right here," were her parting words. Bill did as he was told, and he waited patiently for his mother to return. Five minutes passed ... then 10 minutes ... 20 minutes .... The minutes turned into hours, but still Bill waited on the curb. He waited for his mother to return until the sun set. He was still waiting when the morning sun broke over the horizon.

For three days six-year-old Bill Wilson waited on that curb for his mother to return. But his mother never returned. Eventually, a member of a local church came by and escorted Bill to a church center, where he lived until he was old enough to move out on his own.

Can you imagine an emotional pain any greater than being rejected by your own mother as a child? I can't. I think you'd agree that any child who experienced such a soul-shattering rejection would have every reason to turn into an angry adult who was unwilling, or unable, to express love.

The Power of Persistence

But Bill Wilson chose to climb the wall of his painful childhood and embrace the abundant life on the other side by starting a children's ministry. The story of Bill Wilson's odyssey to open a children's ministry is a study in the power of persistence, for his mission was rife with "insurmountable" walls that he found a way around, over, or through.

He began his mission in the Midwest, and then decided to organize a Sunday school program for children in one of the poorest pockets of Brooklyn. His first stop was an Hispanic church, but after a few weeks, he was asked to leave because the rowdy children were taking too big a toll on the facility.

He persuaded a large Baptist church to house his children's ministry, and they greeted Bill with open arms. Everything was going along fine until a few children broke the pew on the first row of the sanctuary. Bill glued the pew back together and thought he had it in good repair for the services on Sunday.

As he was preaching at the Sunday evening service, he noticed that two women were seated at the repaired end of the pew, and it was holding up beautifully, so he felt pretty proud of himself. But halfway through his sermon, he looked up and saw, to his horror, the largest woman he had ever seen coming through the back door. You can imagine what he was thinking in the middle of his sermon: "Please, please sit anywhere but the front pew!"

The woman passed by the back pews ... kept moving past the middle pews ... and then headed straight for the broken front pew, where she sat down next to the two women. The pew snapped like a dry twig, and all three women crashed to the floor in a heap! Bill recalls, "At that moment I knew my ministry at that church was finished."

Still More Walls

Undeterred, Bill rented an abandoned warehouse in the middle of winter, but he had to send the children home because the landlord had neglected to tell Bill that the warehouse had no heat!

He sought out another warehouse to rent. The owner wasn't too excited about renting the building, but he was willing to sell it for $150,000 if Bill would put $25,000 down within the week. Well, Bill didn't have any money, and he didn't know what he was going to do. Miraculously, Bill received two invitations to speak before large congregations about his children's ministry, and he received a total of $27,000 in offerings. He had enough for his deposit!

But Bill's travails were only just beginning. Bill and a host of volunteers began making repairs and improvements to the warehouse, and everyone was delighted with the progress. Then the warehouse owner decided the building was worth more than the price he and Bill had agreed to. So the owner decided to call in the loan immediately, knowing that Bill couldn't get a loan from a bank. He gave Bill only a few weeks to round up the remainder of the money.

This was one wall that Bill thought he could never climb. But one evening a minister called and suggested Bill raise the money by producing a video of his mission and asking for donations. Bill responded, "I don't have any money to make a video. I can't even pay the bills I have."

To make a long story short, within days Bill received a phone call which led to the opportunity for Bill to produce a video about his mission — for free! Bill sent copies of his video across the country, and he received over $110,000 in donations! He had the money to buy the warehouse.

Thanks to Bill Wilson's undying faith and unshakable perseverance, today he oversees the largest Sunday school program in the United States. During the week he buses in 18,000 children to his mission and provides them with food, fellowship, mentors, and a safe place away from home, a place to learn that somebody cares about them.

Overcoming Humiliation

Like Bill Wilson, Hiram grew up in a loveless household, too. He never saw his mother shed a tear. His father was always cold and harsh.

Hiram's greatest fear in life was that he might become what his father already considered him to be — a failure. At the age of 17, weighing only 120 pounds, Hiram enrolled in the United States Military Academy. He didn't want to attend the Military Academy. In fact, he despised the Military Academy, but he dared not defy his father's will.

At first he performed poorly in his studies, but, as he settled in, his grades gradually improved, and by the time he graduated, his grade point ranked just below the middle of his class.

Shortly after graduation, he returned to his hometown wearing his military uniform. To his embarrassment, when he arrived, the people of his community laughed at him! They just couldn't accept a "failure" like Hiram as a soldier. This humiliating reception left a profound impression upon Hiram for the rest of his life. Even years later, after he became a three-star general, Hiram felt uncomfortable wearing a uniform. Consequently, whenever he could he wore a T-shirt with three stars sewn onto each shoulder rather than his dress uniform.

Getting Past Your Past

Eventually Hiram rose above the sneers and ridicule he received from his family and "friends," and he rose to the highest rank in the military when he was appointed the leader of the Union Army.

And what a leader he became. For, you see, Hiram is known to us today as Ulysses S. Grant, the great general of the Union Army who later became president of the United States!

Hiram experienced humiliation. He experienced rejection. He experienced failure. But because he refused to define himself by the pitfalls of his past, because he forgave his tormentors and forgot his failures, Ulysses S. Grant was able to reach down deep inside himself and unleash his full potential!

Letting Go of Anger

What happens when we don't forgive and forget? The best way to answer that question is to tell you a true episode involving David Cone when he was a starting pitcher for the New York Mets, and what happened to him as a result of his not letting go of a past hurt. You judge for yourself whether the consequences justified his behavior.

The incident occurred late in a crucial game between the Mets and the Atlanta Braves. Cone was on the mound, and there were runners on second and third base. The batter hit a ground ball to the first baseman, who was forced to leave the bag in order to field the ball. This meant that Cone had to run from the pitcher's mound to cover first base.

Cone caught the ball on the run and stepped on first base, but the umpire called the runner safe, insisting that Cone's foot missed the bag. Cone couldn't believe the call. With his back to home plate, Cone began arguing furiously with the first base umpire.

Engrossed in his argument with the umpire, Cone failed to notice that the runners on second and third were advancing to home plate. Both runners scored safely, and the Mets went on to lose the game by two runs — two runs that could have been avoided if only Cone had been able to forgive and forget.

So it is with life. You see, when we're unable to forgive, when we're unable to forget, quite often we compound the damage that has already been done. Our ability to experience forgiveness enables us to transform our blemishes and our shortcomings into something good. An important aspect of moving beyond a rock and a hard place, then, is learning to forget what's behind us — and learning to forgive others for hurting us in the past.

Sometimes we get stuck in the past. Sometimes, emotionally, we become grounded in the past. Sometimes we don't grieve appropriately, and we're unable to let go of the past. But we must climb the wall of the past because when we let it hold us back, we can't become all that we've been created to become.

Be Thankful for Your Blessings

My wife lost her father when she was only 14 years old. As you can imagine, it was a very difficult time for her and for her entire family. But her approach to handling her grief was to thank God for the 14 years that she had a wonderful father.

By taking a positive approach to a great loss, my wife found it much easier to move forward and to provide support and strength to others in her family. Some individuals, however, approach loss of loved ones and friends with anger. And, if they're never able to move beyond their anger, it severely limits their ability to develop relationships of depth and love in the future, always fearing that these relationships may be lost, too.

PRINCIPLE 2: CONQUER YOUR COMPLACENCY

The second principle that the parable of the Four Lepers teaches us is that we can't stay where we are in life. One of the greatest dangers in life is to find ourselves caught between a rock and a hard place and to do nothing about it. It is then, when we do nothing, that we find that our lives become stagnant, and we cease to be productive and to experience the joy in life.

The business world is full of examples of companies that go out of business because they fail to conquer their complacency. The demise of the Baldwin Locomotive Works, at one time the world leader in the manufacture of steam locomotives, is a classic example of a company that remained complacent and failed to adjust to change.

Smith-Corona is a fairly recent example of just such a company. Here's what happened. For more than a century the Smith-Corona Corporation was one of the world's leading typewriter manufacturers. In the early '80s, however, Smith-Corona found themselves caught between a rock and a hard place, for personal computers were starting to cut into their sales.

During the decade of the '80s, 25 million computers entered the U.S. market, and because word processing made it far easier to produce written documents, typewriter sales took a dive.

Smith-Corona, of course, wanted to keep things the way they had always been. They refused to change their core business to keep up with the times, and, as a consequence, in 1995, after 110 years of being one of the most respected names in their industry, the Smith-Corona Corporation filed for bankruptcy.

Easier to Change Yourself Than Others

The key to conquering complacency is to work on yourself, not others. It's a lot easier to change your own behavior than it is to change other people's behavior, that's for sure! The story of the Baldwin Locomotive Works is proof of this principle.

As I pointed out earlier, at one time Baldwin was the world's largest manufacturer of steam locomotives. But times change, and when diesel locomotives came on the production line, Baldwin Locomotive Works refused to change with the times. Instead, they tried to change other people's opinions by spending thousands of dollars purchasing full-page layouts in magazines during the 1940s.

The theme of the their ads was, "Steam Is Here To Stay." As we all know today, steam wasn't here to stay, and the once mighty Baldwin Locomotive Works is now gone with the wind. They became so mired in their complacency that they chose to engage in comfortable self-deception and do nothing to adapt to a changing world. The end result? The company died.

41

The sad saga of the Baldwin Locomotive Works teaches us that it's absolutely essential for us to move beyond our comfort zones and to take risks in life if we seek personal maturation and growth. Why? Because there is nothing so constant as change, and when we're unable to deal with change, we get left behind in life, just like Smith-Corona and Baldwin. But when we realize that we can't stay behind the wall of wishful thinking, then we seek to force open new doors of opportunity.

Put Your Imagination to Work

I'm convinced that if the leaders of Smith-Corona and Baldwin Locomotive had spent as much time thinking of creative ways to adapt to change rather than wallowing in denial, they could have turned their companies around. Likewise, if we're serious about conquering the walls of adversity in our lives, we have to build the doors with our creativity — doors can't build themselves, that's for sure!

One of my favorite stories about creative problem-solving concerns the famous English art critic, John Ruskin, who was a talented artist in his own right.

Ruskin met a wealthy friend for dinner one evening, and his friend arrived all upset. It seems that on the way to the meeting, an ink pen had broken in his friend's breast pocket, leaking indelible India ink onto an expensive handkerchief that the man had recently received as a gift.

The dinner companion removed the handkerchief and showed it to Ruskin. Sure enough, there was a round, black ink stain precisely in the middle of the fabric. The man was so distraught over the stain that he barely touched his dinner, and in his haste to return home, he left the handkerchief on the table.

Ruskin took the handkerchief home with him. Several weeks later the wealthy friend received a package hand-delivered to his home. Much to his surprise, and delight, the man opened the package to find that his ink-stained handkerchief had been transformed into a stunning work of art! Ruskin had taken some India ink, and, using the round stain as the centerpoint, drew an intricate design that covered the entire handkerchief.

I love this story because it shows how people can turn disasters into triumph if they will only think positively and act creatively. Ruskin conquered complacency by building a door in the wall of a friend's minor grievance, and in the process, he enriched both their lives with his selfless expression of esteem and affection for a dear friend.

There's No Time Like the Present

Many times when we find ourselves between a rock and a hard place, we stay where we are by manufacturing excuses. We say, "Well, I'm going to move ahead with my life when I come up with an appropriate plan or an appropriate strategy." But, day after day goes by, and we just never get around to dealing with the problem.

John Wesley, the father of Methodism, was a fiery character, and there was nothing that fired him up more than a religious movement that was popular during his day called the Quietest Movement.

The Quietists believed that since God was all-powerful, He would tell the faithful what to do and when to do it. So the Quietists sat around and prayed all day, waiting for God to tell them what to do. As a result, they never did anything!

Well, even though the Quietest Movement is dead, I still see a lot of people today who are practicing their wait-and-see philosophy. Wesley was a man of action, and his philosophy, like mine, ran totally contrary to the Quietists.

His attitude was this: God has given you a brain; God has given you gifts, talents, and abilities; God has given you a calling to minister in His name to those in need; there are needs in the church and in the world; and, therefore, those needs are your calling to ministry. So let's pray ... and LET'S DO!

PRINCIPLE 3: ACQUIESCE TO ABUNDANCE

And that brings us to the third point: If we can't go back into the past, and we can't stay where we are, then it only stands to reason that we must move forward. And that's what the four lepers did. If they wanted to survive, they had no alternative but to go into the Syrian camp.

The lepers, you see, were able to enjoy an abundance of food and supplies because they moved forward. Likewise, abundance is available to all of us if only we will become like the lepers and seek it out! The Bible says, *"Seek and ye shall find,"* doesn't it? It doesn't say, "Stay where you are, and you'll get what you need." It says SEEK AND YOU WILL FIND. The first step in acquiescing to abundance, then, is to SEEK it out!

Are You a Self-Opening Gate?

Many years ago you could drive along a country road and come upon what was referred to as a self-opening gate. If you stopped your car too far in front of the gate, the gate wouldn't open. If, however, you drove all the way up to the gate before stopping, the metal springs buried underneath the road would activate the gate, and the gate would open so you could drive through.

In many ways, life is the same way. When we drive right up to our problems and don't stop until we are face to face with them, more often than not, a gate will swing open, and we'll be free to drive through. But when we are tentative, or when we stop before we even bother to confront our problems, they never go away. We can only go over or through the walls in our lives when we challenge them.

Get Used to Having Problems

As a counselor I often meet with people who are looking for me to help them solve one big problem in their lives. They seem to think that if only they had more money or if only their spouse was more this or that, then life would be a cakewalk.

But guess what? Once their major problem has been resolved, a month or so later I see the same people again, asking me to help them with their next big problem.

The point is that problem-solving is an on going process, for as soon as you solve one, there's a couple of more to take its place. The key to living the abundant life isn't to eradicate the problems in our lives. The key to abundance is to get better at solving the problems we have, because as long as we draw a breath in this life, we will surely be confronted with problems.

It's like Clarence Thomas said when he accepted the position as a member of the United States Supreme Court. "You may not like me," he quipped. "But that's too bad. I'm going to be here a long time, *so get used to it.*"

You and I are going to have problems for a long time, my friend, so we might as well get used to it!

What Have You Done Since?

The need to keep struggling to overcome our problems reminds me of the story about a group of military officers who approached

Napoleon with the request that he promote a certain enlisted man.

Napoleon inquired as to why the officers felt the soldier was worthy of a promotion. The officers told Napoleon that the soldier's cleverness and courage had enabled the French Army to win an important victory in a battle just several days before. Napoleon pondered the request for a few seconds before responding with this question:

"What has the man done since?"

To this question the officers had no answer. Napoleon knew that all too often a little-known soldier will demonstrate a sudden burst of brilliance and help to WIN A BATTLE or two. But Napoleon understood that the soldiers who WIN THE WAR are those individuals who are always moving forward, always forging ahead, always climbing their walls, day in and day out.

Step Out and Take a Risk

Burke Hedges, in his best-selling book, *You Can't Steal Second with Your Foot on First*, observes that if we're going to move ahead in life, we need to be willing to take a few risks.

Hedges argues that there's a big difference between risk and gambling. In gambling, if you take $1,000 and you put it down on the roulette table, you're either going to double it or you're going to get nothing. But the outcome is out of your control.

You take a risk, on the other hand, when you invest your money in the stock market. The market is a risk because you stand a slim chance of losing it all. But you also stand a good chance of getting at least a 10% return over time. By investing your money wisely, you mitigate your risks, and you increase the likelihood that your investment will increase over the long haul.

The beauty of taking risks is that you're in control. If your investments start to lose money, Hedges observes, you can always sell the stock and cut your losses. That's why you're wise to take *calculated risks*, but foolish to take *reckless gambles*.

The same principle holds true for the rest of our lives. Abundance can be ours if we take calculated risks and move beyond a rock and a hard place, much like the four lepers did. The story of the four lepers teaches us that when we're caught between a rock and a hard place, we can't go back and we can't stay where we are. The only way out is to confront our problems and move ahead.

When it's all said and done, where we end up in life isn't determined so much by our circumstances. Where we end up in life is determined by *how we choose to respond to those circumstances.*

REVIEW

How often in life do we feel as though we've lost control? How often do we spend more time kissing other people's mules and dancing to other people's music than being about what we want to be about? It doesn't have to be like that!

Principle 1: Avoid the pitfalls of the past

First of all, the story of the four lepers tells us that we can't go back. How often do we seek to live in the past? How often do we long for the way things once were?

When World War I broke out, President Woodrow Wilson said, "We shall be neutral in name and in fact." But that's not the way life is. When the whole world around you is at war, you can't be neutral and at peace. And the American people learned that valuable lesson the hard way.

Principle 2: Conquer your complacency

The second principle that we learn from the four lepers is that we can't stay where we are in life. The greatest danger in life is to find ourselves between a rock and a hard place and to do nothing.

When we do nothing in the face of our problems, then we resign ourselves to going nowhere, and we cease being productive and are unable to experience the simple joys of abundance.

Principle 3: Acquiesce to abundance

And that brings us to the third point: We can't go back into the past and we can't stay where we are ... which means we can only move forward. And that's what the four lepers did.

Once the lepers made their decision and committed themselves to action, they were free to enjoy the abundance of the deserted camp.

CHAPTER 4

~

CAPTURING THE VISION

In the long run, we only hit what we aim at. There-
fore, though we might fail immediately, we had bet-
ter aim at something high.
— Henry David Thoreau

The most pathetic person in the world is someone
who has sight, but has no vision.
— Helen Keller

Near the turn of the 20th century, an energetic young man named Frank secured a job as a clerk in a hardware store. As he learned the business, he saw that there were thousands of items in the store which the customers seldom asked for. He knew it didn't make sense to keep this outdated inventory, for it was taking up valuable shelf space.

He proposed to his boss that they hold a sale and clear some of it out. The boss reluctantly agreed to a small sale. Frank marked the outdated inventory down to 10 cents. The sale was such a success that the boss agreed to a second sale. It, too, was a tremendous success.

Vision of a "Five and Ten Cent" Store

This gave Frank the idea of starting a store that sold items that cost either a nickel or a dime. The clerk approached his boss with the idea that he would run this new "five and ten cent" store if the boss would put up the capital.

The boss flatly refused on the grounds that it wouldn't work. Naturally, the clerk was disappointed, but he was convinced his vision of a "five and ten cent" store would work. Several years later he managed to save enough money to start the store on his own.

To make a long story short, Frank's first store became a huge success, and he expanded his vision until he had opened thousands of stores all across the United States and Canada.

You see, Frank became better known as F. W. Woolworth, and his chain of five and ten cent stores — Woolworth's — became a household name in the early to mid-1900s and made him one of the wealthiest men in America.

Capturing a Vision

I tell you this story to illustrate the power of capturing a vision. Frank had the vision to see his successful five and ten cent store long before he had the money to start it up. And he had the vision to see thousands of these stores all across the continent long before the concept of a retail chain store even existed.

His boss, on the other hand, lacked vision. All he could see was the here and now — namely, a little hardware store on the corner of Main Street, USA. His lack of vision cost him the opportunity to share in the enormous profits of the Woolworth empire.

YOUR VISION: THE GATEWAY TO LIFE

We are setting ourselves up for disappointment and failure if we set sail in life without a plan or a vision. We must take time and develop our vision, because without a vision, we don't know where we're headed and are, therefore, pre-ordaining our defeat.

If we have a vision, on the other hand, we can determine both the direction we will take in life and the height of our success. In times of adversity, we can muster the courage to climb the walls in our way because in our "mind's eye" we can see the big picture, and we know the prize at the end is worth the struggle to get there.

That's why I say your vision is your gateway to life. When you have a big, clear vision, you don't see the walls in your life as impasses. You see them as "gates" that have to be negotiated so you can stay on course. That's what Stephen Covey, author of the best-selling *7 Habits of Highly Successful People*, means when he talks about "starting with the end in mind." If you start knowing ahead of time where you will end up, you'll find a means to get there, one way or the other.

Visions Borne from Adversity

One of life's greatest ironies is the fact that some of the grandest visions are borne out of adversity, proving once again that when one door closes, another door opens. Take a look at this list of some famous visionaries who molded their visions from the ashes of adversity:

- An inventor witnesses the death of children due to contaminated milk and *envisions* a method to preserve milk. His name was Gail Borden, founder of Borden's Milk and Ice Cream.

- A widower with a son loses his job at a department store and *envisions* the day when he will own his own store and be his own boss. His name? George Kinney, founder and president of Kinney Shoes.

- Two life-long entrepreneurs start a business in the basement of their homes with a *vision* of revitalizing free enterprise throughout the world. Their names? Rich DeVos and Jay Van Andel, the co-founders of the Amway Corporation.

- A young athlete living in a government-funded housing project in Pennsylvania *envisions* escaping the misery of the coal mines by becoming a football star. His name is Mike Ditka, a pro football Hall of Fame inductee and head coach of the New Orleans Saints.

- Two tinkerers set up a shop in a garage with the *vision* of growing a business that is on the cutting edge of the information age. Their names? William Hewlett and David Packard of Hewlett-Packard Information Systems.

- In the 1800s a young man realizes that people are dying following surgery due to unsanitary conditions. He convinces his two brothers to *capture his vision* of producing sterile bandages. Their names? Robert, Edward, and James Johnson of Johnson & Johnson Health Care Products.

- A young man's older brother is shot down in World War II, and the younger brother eases his loneliness by listening to the radio. He *envisions* himself one day becoming a radio announcer. His name? Dick Clark, world-famous radio and TV announcer and host of *American Bandstand.*

- A general practitioner *envisions* himself performing a surgical procedure that everyone says can't be done. His time is limited because he suffers from rheumatoid arthritis which one day will prevent him from operating. His name? Dr. Christiaan Barnard, the surgeon who performed the first successful human heart transplant.

These examples — and thousands more like them that occur every day of the week — prove that great things are accomplished as the consequence of great visions, and that great visions can crystallize out of adversity if people are willing to climb the walls in their lives.

Never Stop Dreaming

An admirer approached Robert Schuller one day, shook his hand vigorously, and said in a sincere effort to praise the minister, "I hope you live to see all your dreams come true."

Schuller looked the man in the eye and responded evenly, "I hope I don't or I will have died before I've died, because you die when you stop dreaming." Schuller understood this fundamental principle: No vision, no future.

Schuller also understood that there are a lot more cynics than optimists in this world, and the only way for optimists to accomplish their dreams is to keep their eyes raised high and focused on the horizon, or they won't be able to see above the nearest wall.

Have you ever noticed how people will go out of their way to tell you that you can't do something? It seems that most people would rather burst your bubble than help you inflate it. If your vision is strong enough, however, it doesn't make any difference what other people say about your dream, because one way or another, you're going to make it happen.

The Boy Whose Dream Came True

One of my favorite stories about the redeeming power of an unshakable vision concerns a man named Marty Roberts. Marty was the son of an itinerant horse trainer. As a result, Marty spent most of his school-age years traveling with his family from one farm to another. His education, as a consequence, was disjointed at best.

He did, however, manage to graduate from high school, and in his senior year, Marty was required to write a paper on his dreams and aspirations for life. He took the assignment very seriously, and he poured his heart out into the paper. He shared his vision for a 200-acre ranch with a 4,000-square-foot house. He even provided diagrams of both. He was as proud of his paper as any school project he had ever completed.

Can you imagine Marty's shock when his paper was returned with a big red "F" scribbled across the top? He immediately approached the teacher, inquiring as to why his paper had received a failing grade.

The teacher told the crestfallen young man that he failed the paper because the content wasn't realistic. After all, the teacher noted, Marty was the son of an itinerant horse trainer. He had no money and no resources. He didn't have the capital to purchase land or to build buildings or to buy horses and breed horses. Which meant, in the teacher's narrow mind, that Marty's paper was more fantasy than reality.

The teacher instructed Marty that in order to get a passing grade, he would have to rewrite the paper. Marty went home and told his parents what had happened and asked for their advice. His father responded, "Marty, it's up to you." The next day Marty told the teacher that he would keep his "F" because he wasn't going to give up his dream.

Fortunately, Marty's vision out-lasted the teacher's cynicism, for today Marty Roberts owns a 200-acre ranch with a 4,000-square-foot home. Mounted over the fireplace in an elegant frame is the seven-page paper in which Marty first described his dream!

Happy Ending Gets Even Happier

If Marty's story ended right here, you'd have to say it was a happy ending. But it gets even better. Marty's vision included love and forgiveness, and to make his vision complete, years later he asked the teacher who gave him the "F" to run a summer camp for youth at Marty's ranch!

The teacher graciously accepted the offer, and the two men healed the breach between them. It wasn't long before the teacher confessed to Marty that he wasn't the only student the teacher had injured with his cynical attitude.

"As a teacher," he confessed, "I've stolen many young people's dreams through the years, and I'm ashamed of it. I've taken away something that would have enabled them to become what they could become. But I praise God that you didn't allow your vision to be taken away."

These two men are living proof that a vision can touch, and change, more than just the person who created it. Marty's vision changed his fortune in the world, but in the process, it also changed a teacher's view of the world, as well as changing the views of hundreds of campers and students who would come under the teacher's influence. That's why I say visions are "gateways to life" — they open up doors of hope and possibility.

A vision is important in that it enables us to transcend *where we are* to see *where we can be*. A vision enables us to transcend our understanding of *who we are* to see *who we can become*. A vision enables us to transcend *what we are* to see *what we can become*.

YOUR VISION: DEPTH FOR THE LONG HAUL

For a vision to endure, it must open gates, but it must also have depth so that it will endure for the long haul. One organization that began as a result of a vision with depth was the Mayo Clinic, which has been ministering to the needs of the sick for over a century.

Begun in 1889 by two visionary brothers, Drs. William and Charles Mayo, the Mayo Clinic is the largest and most famous medical clinic in the world. The clinic has long been known as the leader in technological advances and surgical breakthroughs. Open-heart surgery and the CAT scan were pioneered at Mayo. Cortisone was developed by two of its staff members, who later received the Nobel Prize for their achievement.

Big Vision with a Big Purpose

What is the secret of their success? Certainly one key was the fact that the founders had a vision with depth. The Mayo brothers weren't looking to get rich by running patients through a "medical mill." They weren't looking to make a splashy name for themselves so they could hobnob with politicians and get their photographs splashed across the Sunday newspaper.

The brothers were looking to create the most advanced treatment and research hospital the world had ever seen. More than 100 years later, the clinic still enjoys the world's best reputation for excellence in medicine and continues to build on the founders' original vision of depth. In 1987 the Mayo Clinic announced a plan for expansion to carry it through the year 2020. The Mayo brothers' vision is alive and well, proving that a vision with depth will endure year after year.

Robert Schuller is another example of a person who created a vision of depth — and who continues to expand on that vision. At age 60, Schuller outlined a 10-year vision for his ministry. When he turned 70, rather than resting on his laurels and "dying before he was really dead," Schuller literally practiced what he preached by outlining his vision for the next 10 years of his ministry!

YOUR VISION: BREADTH TO AVOID TUNNEL VISION

Because they dared to create a vision with depth, the Mayo brothers and Robert Schuller have built hugely successful enterprises, one to minister to people's physical needs and the other to minister to their spiritual needs.

But in order for a worthwhile vision to survive, it must also have breadth. By breadth I mean the vision can't be so narrowly focused that it ignores how it fits in with the rest of the world. "Tunnel vision" is doomed to fail because it doesn't take into account how it will fit in with the "Big Picture."

To illustrate what I mean, I'd like to tell you a story about a large health care company that developed a new toothbrush in the 1980s. The toothbrush was an instant success, and it captured a large portion of the market within a couple of years.

In order to achieve brand recognition and product visibility on the retail shelf, the manufacturer provided the retail stores with complimentary display racks that featured their toothbrush. These racks were made of plastic with square grids in which the toothbrushes were placed.

Then one day a recent MBA graduate in the marketing department came up with a plan to reduce the cost of manufacturing the racks. He calculated that the company could save $50,000 a year by manufacturing racks with open slots in the back of each rack, as opposed to a solid back.

The company adopted the MBA's cost-saving proposal without first running it by the field representatives who placed the racks in the retail outlets. Hundreds of thousands of the new open-back racks were manufactured, and the reps were instructed to throw out the old racks and replace them with the new ones.

The Results of Short-Sighted Vision

The complaints about the new racks began almost immediately! It seems that many of the premium toothbrushes were packaged in long, rectangular boxes, and, yes, they fit perfectly into the square grids of the new toothbrush racks. But some toothbrushes were not packaged in boxes and were only wrapped in cellophane. The cellophane wrapped toothbrushes were too small for the openings, and as a result, they kept falling through the open slots in the back.

Since retailers could only use the racks for toothbrushes that came in a box, they were understandably upset, and they demanded the company remove the new racks and replace them with the old ones. Unfortunately, almost every one of the old racks had been discarded, just as the company ordered.

In the end, the company had to throw out the new racks, re-manufacture 50,000 of the original racks, and then re-install them all across the country, which ended up costing the company millions of dollars in expensive production costs, lost time, and bad will on the part of retailers and customers.

This is a perfect example of what can happen if a vision lacks breadth. The idea of a less expensive rack sounded good to management, but because they didn't consider the impact of the racks on the "big picture," it ended up costing even more money, instead of saving money.

The lesson is clear: If a person's vision is so narrowly conceived that it hurts people more than it helps them, he or she needs to rethink the vision. What is expedient today may sound the death knell for the future.

YOUR VISION: HEIGHT TO STRETCH YOUR HORIZONS

If we are to overcome the walls of adversity in life, we must have a vision with sufficient height, for what good does it do to win the battle and lose the war? The individual with a lofty vision, however, is the one who can lose lots of battles — and yet recover and still win the war.

Tommy Lasorda, the legendary manager of the Los Angeles Dodgers, enjoys telling the story of how he raised the height of his team's vision when he was coaching in the minor leagues.

It was 1971, and Lasorda's team had just lost their seventh straight game. During that same time period, sportswriters all across the country were asked to name the greatest major league team in the history of baseball, and the honor went to the 1927 Yankees.

Lasorda's team was heading back into the locker room after their latest loss. They were shuffling along with their heads down, looking every bit like beaten puppies. Lasorda decided the team needed a good pep talk.

Just Like the '27 Yankees

"I don't ever want to see you fellows with your heads down again," he shouted at his disheartened team in the locker room. "Just because you aren't winning right now doesn't mean you're not a great team. You're going to start winning! As you know, the sportswriters voted the 1927 Yankees the greatest team in the history of Major League Baseball. Well, the Yankees lost nine straight games in 1927, too — just like you guys!"

Lasorda's pep talk worked. Almost overnight the players lifted their heads. Their attitudes changed. They started winning game after game. By the end of the season, they were the league champs.

One day Mrs. Lasorda asked, "Tommy, are you sure the '27 Yankees lost nine straight games?"

"How would I know? Tommy responded. *"I was only one year old at the time. But it made the point!"*

The point that Lasorda made was that if you want to improve your results, you need to raise your vision. As a wise person once observed, "If you shoot for the stars and miss, you'll end up on the moon. But if you shoot for the top of the fence and miss, you may end up with a fistful of mud." That's why it's better to aim too high and miss, rather than aim too low and hit.

YOUR VISION: COUNT THE COST

Jesus advised people to dream big dreams, but to be realistic about the price they would have to pay to make those dreams happen. He knew full well that you don't get something for nothing in this world, or in any other world, for that matter.

Jesus said, "For which of you, desiring to build a tower, does not first sit down and count the cost, whether he has enough to complete it? Otherwise, when he has laid a foundation, and is not able to finish, all who see it begin to mock him, saying, 'This man began to build, and was not able to finish.'"

Several important principles are lifted up in this story concerning how we should approach life, the first being "Don't start what you can't finish." It's only common sense that before you go out to buy a car, you need to calculate how much you can spend on a monthly payment and then look for a car in that price range. The same goes for buying a house. If you can only afford a $100,000 home, there's no sense in looking at $200,000 homes because you're just setting yourself up for disappointment.

Just as there is a price to pay in dollars and cents for cars and homes, there is also a price to pay in time and effort if we're serious about making our dreams come true. We shouldn't set ourselves up for disappointment if we're not willing to do what it takes to get the job done.

Fable of the Three Little Pigs

When my son Chaz was little, one of his favorite stories was the fable of the Three Little Pigs. The story, though simple, provides an important lesson for children that many adults need to be reminded of from time to time.

As you will recall, the three little pigs were leaving home and each set out to build his own house. The first two pigs were not particularly concerned about the quality of their houses. They just wanted some shelter from the harsh weather. One built his home of straw and the other of wood.

The third little pig, however, built his home of bricks so that it would be strong and safe and ward off any impending dangers. As it turns out, it was a good thing that he did, because the big, bad wolf came and blew down the house of straw and the house of wood. But the three little pigs found safety in the house built of bricks.

The point is you can't build a brick house on a straw or wood house "budget." A brick house takes more effort. It takes more time. And it takes more money. But in the long run, the brick house is worth the price you paid because it endures.

There is a cost attached to every vision, and quite often the price we're willing to pay will determine the quality of our experience in seeing our vision fulfilled. The story of the Three Little Pigs reminds us that anything worth doing is worth doing well.

The "Cost" of The *Scarlet Letter*

The great American author, Nathaniel Hawthorne, was born with tremendous creativity, and he had a burning desire to write a novel. He didn't earn much money as a civil servant, however, and he struggled mightily to provide for the basic needs for himself and his wife.

One day Hawthorne came home early from his job at the Customs House. He'd been fired. He said to his wife, "I'm a failure. I've let you down. I've let myself down. I don't have a job anymore, and I can't provide for us anymore."

"Oh, Nathaniel, that's fine," his faithful wife, Sophia, responded. "Now you can go ahead and write that book that you've always been wanting to write."

"How will we support ourselves?" Hawthorne implored.

"All these years that you've been giving me money to care for the house, I've been setting aside as much as I could," Sophia replied. "I've managed to save up enough so that you can write for a year." Because of his wife's sacrifice, Nathaniel Hawthorne was able to write a literary classic, *The Scarlet Letter*.

Sophia Hawthorne knew that there was a price to pay if she truly wanted to see her husband's vision realized. So she "counted the cost" and did what she had to do to set it aside.

The truth of the matter is this: Those who seek to get by in life by doing as little as they can will get out of life about as much as they put in. The individual who has a vision with depth and breadth and height can't attain that vision unless that individual is willing to count the cost.

No doubt about it, you reap what you sow. That principle is as true today as it was when it was first uttered, thousands of years ago.

YOUR VISION: MOVING BEYOND YOUR COMFORT ZONE

Creating a vision is not for the timid or faint of heart. It takes courage to dream big dreams, that's for sure. But people who choose to "play it safe" by refusing to imagine a world beyond the comfort zone of their TV sets are really just kidding themselves, for there is no comfort in the comfort zone.

To better explain what I mean, I'd like to tell you the fable of the Two Seeds. Two little seeds were planted in the fertile soil of spring.

"I want to grow," one of the seeds said. And soon that seed began to shoot its roots deep into the earth and its sprouts upward through the crust of the soil. It opened its arms and heart to spring, and before long its buds began to blossom. It began to feel the warmth of the sun upon its face and the morning dew on its petals. It was growing and happy and proud.

The other seed said, "I'm not sure I want to grow. I don't want to send my roots down because I can't see where they're going. And I don't want to send my sprouts up through the crusty soil, for they might get damaged on the way. If I allow my buds to burst forth and blossom, some child may come and pluck me up. So I think I'll just lie here and wait and see what happens."

One day a rooster walked by the two seeds. He cocked his head to the side and admired the growing seed. Then the rooster scratched at the soil, saw the ungrown seed — and ate it.

The fable reminds us that if we aren't willing to move forward, if we aren't willing to grow, if we aren't willing to risk ourselves, we'll be swallowed up by life.

We can't stay where we are, frozen in time. We must be moving forward or backward. Moving forward takes effort, because you have to struggle to get up the hill. Moving backward, on the other hand, is much easier because the only way we can coast in life is downhill. Personally, I'd rather struggle and move up hill a little than coast and move downhill a lot. How about you?

YOUR VISION: COURAGE TO PERSEVERE

Finally, the individual who learns to confront the walls of adversity in life is the individual who not only has a vision and is willing to pay the price of achieving it, but is also the individual who perseveres. When it comes to climbing walls and building doors, persistence overcomes resistance every time.

That's why visions are so important — when we have a strong vision, we can visualize in our minds the light at the end of the tunnel long before we see the actual light. A strong vision keeps us moving forward in the darkness because we know it's just a matter of time before we arrive at our goal.

This principle reminds me of a true-life event that happened to a long-distance swimmer named Florence Chadwick. It was the Fourth of July, 1952, and the 34-year-old woman (who had already been the first person to swim the English Channel in both directions) set out to swim the 21-mile stretch between Catalina Island and California.

If she accomplished the task, she would be the first woman to do so. Millions were watching on television as she made her way through the numbing cold waters and thick fog. Several times her crew had to fire rifles to scare off the sharks. As the hours ticked by, the bone-chilling cold of the water was beginning to take its toll. Fatigue wasn't the biggest challenge to overcome in this swim — it was the bone-chilling cold of the water.

Defeated by Fog

Florence's mother and trainer urged her on, assuring her that land wasn't far off. But the thick fog prevented her from seeing the shoreline, and, consequently, she asked her crew to help her out of the water 15 hours and 55 minutes after she had started her swim. What she didn't know was she was only half a mile away from land when she quit!

As her body began to warm, the reality of her failure began to set in. She blurted out to one reporter, "Look, I'm not excusing myself, but if I could have seen land, I might have made it."

You see, she didn't fail because of the wall of fatigue, or even because of the wall of the numbing cold waters. She failed because the fog prevented her from seeing her goal. If there were no fog that day, she would have kept on going.

Fortunately, Florence's story has a happy ending. Two months later she swam the same course and completed it. The fog was thick on that day, too, but her faith was intact because her vision wasn't obscured. In fact, she not only became the first woman to swim the

Catalina Channel, she also beat the men's record by over two hours!

Never Give up

One of the great principles of mastering defeat is not to allow defeat to defeat you. Below is a list of one man's failures. As you read this list, see if you can guess who this person is. The chronology of this man's life is irrefutable evidence that there is no shame in getting knocked down — the only shame is not getting back up again.

1831 - *failed* in business
1832 - *defeated* for state legislature
1833 - *failed* in business again
1834 - elected to state legislature
1835 - *sweetheart died*
1836 - *had a nervous breakdown*
1838 - *defeated* for speaker
1840 - *defeated* for elector
1843 - *defeated* for Congress
1846 - elected to Congress
1848 - *defeated* for Congress
1855 - *defeated* for Senate
1856 - *defeated* for vice-president
1858 - *defeated* for Senate

Who was this "failure" who set himself up for defeat year after year? He was the man who in 1860 was elected President of the United States. He was Abraham Lincoln.

Abraham Lincoln refused to allow defeat to defeat him. His personal vision was so strong that it enabled him to persevere, year in and year out, until he saw his vision fulfilled. Lincoln understood that quitting was NOT an option, and his life's accomplishments are a testimony to the power of perserverance.

We all have a lot to learn from Abraham Lincoln's example. Now I'd like to share with you a little poem with a big message, for it captures the essence of Lincoln's fighting spirit.

You'll Do It

Somebody said that it couldn't be done,
  But he with a chuckle replied
That "maybe" it couldn't but he would be the one
  Who wouldn't say so 'til he'd tried.

So he buckled right in, with a trace of a grin on his face.
    If he worried he hid it.
He started to sing as he tackled the thing
    That couldn't be done, but he did it.
Somebody scoffed: "Oh, you'll never do that,
    At least no one has ever done it."
But he took off his coat and he took off his hat,
    And the first thing we knew he'd begun it;
With a lift of his chin, and a bit of a grin,
    Without any doubt or quibbling.
He started to sing as he tackled the thing
    That couldn't be done, and he did it.
There are thousands to tell you it cannot be done;
    There are thousands to prophesy failure;
There are thousands to point out to you, one by one,
    The dangers that wait to assail you;
But just buckle in with a bit of a grin,
    Then take off your coat and go to it;
Just start in to sing as you tackle the thing
    That "cannot be done"— and you'll do it.

REVIEW

As we confront adversity in life, we will no doubt experience both times of joy and sorrow, times of victory and defeat. A strong vision enables us to overcome the setbacks because we can "see" the big picture, and we know the prize at the end is worth the struggle. I call your vision the "gateway to life" because it opens the door to what you *can become*, rather than to what you already are.

Depth for the long haul

For a vision to endure, it must have depth for the long haul. If a vision is powerful enough, it can literally endure for generations.

Breadth to avoid "tunnel vision"

A vision needs to have breadth so that it can fit comfortably into the world at large. If a vision is too narrowly focused, it can end up hurting more people than it helps.

Height to stretch your horizons

A vision must have height, for what good does it do to win the battle but lose the war. When it's all said and done, it's better to aim too high and miss than to aim too low and hit.

Count the cost

Everything in life has a cost attached to it. If you're serious about making your dreams come true, you have to "count the cost" of success ahead of time and then be willing to pay the price in time and effort.

Moving beyond your comfort zone

Creating a vision is not for the timid or faint of heart. It takes courage to dream big dreams, but in the end we must move forward, for the only direction we can coast in life is downhill.

Courage to persevere

One of the great principles in mastering defeat is not to allow defeat to defeat you. Every successful person knows, *persistence beats resistance — and quitting is NEVER an option!*

PART 2

~

Climbing the Wall
or Building a Door

*Kites rise highest against the wind —
not with it.*
> — Winston Churchill

*Not knowing when the dawn will come,
I open every door.*
> — Emily Dickinson

CHAPTER 5

﹏

POSITIONING YOURSELF

*There is one quality more important than know-how.
This is know-how by which we determine not only
how to accomplish our purposes, but what our purposes are to be.*

— Norber Wiener, scientist

Every fall, as the new school year begins, many of us parents attend open houses at the schools where our children or grandchildren are students. On one occasion I attended an open house where the principal shared an interesting story about a man who started three companies with rather strange names.

One company was called, *"I don't care."* Another company was called, *"It doesn't matter."* And the third was called, *"Anyone will be fine."*

Why would a businessman name his companies such odd names, you may ask? Well, he definitely had a method to his madness. You see, the man was in the long distance phone business, and he knew that every time people change addresses, they must sign up for new phone service. While they're being signed up, the service representative asks them what long distance phone carrier they would like to use.

Many people will request AT&T, Sprint, MCI, or the like. But the people without a preference will usually give one of three responses: *"I don't care," "It doesn't matter,"* or *"Anyone will be fine."* The businessman reasoned that when someone responded with one of these three answers, they would automatically become one of his customers.

Little Things Can Make a Big Difference

The customers who gave one of these responses soon found out the hard way that they SHOULD HAVE cared, for it turns out that the businessman's companies were charging exorbitant fees for their long distance service.

For example, a long distance directory assistance call, which was costing around 50 cents with the major carriers, was costing $17.00 with the new carrier, nearly 34 times the normal rate!

The school official who told the story went on to note how even our small decisions can make a big difference. The implications for education were, of course, quite clear. Some subjects in school may not appear to be important; the amount of time your kids spend doing their homework may not appear to be important; and getting your children to school on time may not appear to be important. But when the children head out into the world to fend for themselves, paying attention to the little things can make a big difference.

The same can be said for our decisions, both large and small. We're confronted with hundreds of decisions every single day, and those decisions play a big part in determining how we position ourselves in this life.

Think about it this way: People who stop by the tavern every night after work are positioning themselves to become alcoholics, isn't that true? What about people who insist on eating junk food all day long? What about people who continue to smoke cigarettes despite the mountain of research that says smoking is bad for you? Aren't they positioning themselves for a host of health problems down the road?

Positioning Yourself on the Field of Life

John Madden, the former professional football coach and current sportscaster for FOX, maintains that a football coach's most valuable tool is a chalkboard. How a coach positions his 11 players on the field will ultimately determine whether his team wins or loses the game. Coaches diagram plays on the chalkboard before the game and during halftime so that the players know where they are supposed to be on the field during any given play.

If players are positioned in the right spot, chances are the play will succeed. If they "miss their assignment" and end up positioning themselves incorrectly, it can result in the team losing the game.

In a similar manner, the way we position ourselves in life may well determine our ability to experience the abundant life. In the words of William Shakespeare, "Men at some time are masters of their fates: The fault, dear Brutus, is not in our stars, but in ourselves." Shakespeare knew that when it was all said and done, the way we position ourselves by the choices we make, both big and small, will determine our fate.

Life Is Like a Game of Checkers

Martin Buber, the noted theologian, compares the proper positioning of your life to the game of checkers. The goal in checkers, of course, is to win the game. Likewise, the goal of life is to "win" the abundant life, and to do so, we must abide by the same rules that regulate the game of checkers.

There are three basic rules in checkers that parallel the proper positioning of ourselves in life. First, you cannot make two moves at once. In a like manner, we must *position ourselves in relationship to our goals and objectives*, for we can only work toward our goals one at a time.

Secondly, you can only move forward. Similarly, we must *position ourselves in the proper relationship to time.*

And thirdly, you must always move toward the last row, for when your checker gets on the last row, you are free to move it in any direction you choose. Likewise, we must always seek the last row in life, which is *positioning ourselves to serve others*, before we are free in the truest sense of the word. And in so doing, we will find the abundant life.

Now let's take a moment to discuss each of these positioning principles in more depth.

POSITIONING OUR LIVES IN RELATION TO OUR GOALS

There's a church in Jacksonville, Florida, that is located at the intersection of two major highways, Interstate 10 and Interstate 95. As a result, the church is a popular place for meetings because it's so easily accessible from all parts of the city.

In my frequent travels to and from the church from all directions, I had the opportunity to see countless hitchhikers who were always thumbing a ride to another destination.

The hitchhikers would hold up signs to help flag down a motorist headed toward their destination. One sign would read, "Miami," while another would read "Tallahassee." Still another would read "New York." On one particular occasion, I passed by a hitchhiker holding a sign that said "Anywhere." He didn't know where he was going, but he knew that he wanted to get out of where he was.

Like the hitchhikers at that intersection in Jacksonville, we, too, arrive at crossroads in our own lives each and every day. Some of us know exactly where we're going because we have clear goals in our lives, so we position ourselves in the direction we want to go and hold up a sign that says "Financial Freedom"... or "Better Health"... or "Happy Family Life."

Sadly, all too many people don't set goals for themselves, and they end up holding signs that say "Anywhere"... "I'll settle for that" ... and "Please help me, I'm clueless." We should feel sorry for these people, because they're positioning themselves for failure.

The Power of Goal-Setting

It's obvious that in order to position yourself for success, you have to know where you're going. It's not rocket science I'm talking about here. It's only common sense. But I'm continually amazed at the number of people who don't take control of the direction of their lives by sitting down and writing down their goals. Positioning yourself so that you can accomplish your goals may be the single most powerful activity you can take to ensure an abundant life.

To illustrate what I mean, I'd like to tell you a story that happened many years ago to Charles Schwab, the president of Bethlehem Steel.

A business consultant named Ivy Lee informed Schwab that he had a simple plan that would enable Schwab to run his business more efficiently, from the top person all the way down to the lowest man on the company totem pole.

Lee was so confident his plan would work that he left his compensation totally up to Schwab. All that Lee asked was for Schwab to send him a check for what he thought his service was worth.

Being a shrewd businessman, Schwab agreed, and Lee revealed his plan. It was simply this: At the beginning of each day, each manager and employee would make a list of things that needed to be done that day and prioritize them in their order of importance. They would then begin working on the first item on the list and wouldn't go to the next item until the previous one had been completed.

As soon as each employee got to his desk each morning, his first task was to take a few minutes and draw up a new list for the day, with the unfinished business from the previous day placed at the top.

This simple exercise forced people to write daily goals and to manage their time more effectively. As a result, within a few months, productivity at Bethlehem Steel skyrocketed, and Schwab sent Lee a check for $25,000 — which was worth 10 times what it's worth today.

You Can't Serve Two Masters

The Bible shares one of the universal principles of life when it states, "No one can serve two masters; for either he will hate the one and love the other, or he will be devoted to one and despise the other." This simple scripture teaches us that if we're to experience the abundant life, then we must be willing to choose where we're going to devote our time and energies in life. In other words, you have to focus on one thing at a time!

Perhaps you remember when Michael Jordan, the tremendous basketball player for the Chicago Bulls, retired from basketball following his father's death in order to play baseball. He drew huge crowds during his stint in the minor leagues, but his mastery of baseball wasn't even close to his mastery of basketball. The greatest basketball player of all time was less than average as a baseball player.

He ended up leaving baseball after a season and a half to return to basketball. Many would agree that his focus on baseball for that brief period took a toll on his basketball skills, at least for the short term, proving once again that you can't serve two masters.

People who grab at straws and clutter their lives with aimless pursuits are destined to remain unfulfilled. In their attempt to achieve all things, they will water down their efforts so much that they'll likely end up attaining nothing.

The Difference Between Being and Having

Over the years I've counseled many people who think they can buy happiness or peace of mind by accumulating material things. These people are often good at setting and achieving their goals, but all too often their goals are shallow, and the satisfaction they get from, say, owning a new boat passes in a matter of days.

Noted educator, Mark Hopkins, would often challenge his university classes to consider the worthiness of their goals and objectives in life. He would begin by challenging his students to answer a series of simple, yet wonderfully enlightening, questions:

"We would all like to have the world," he would say, "as much of it as we want. But consider this: Would you be willing to have the world, as much of it as you wanted, and be deaf? You might answer 'yes.'

"Would you be willing to have the world, as much of it as you wanted, and be deaf and blind? It's unlikely, but you still might answer 'yes.'

"Would you be willing to have the world, as much of it as you wanted, and be deaf and blind and dumb? You would certainly answer 'no,' for there comes the time in such reckoning when you must face the issue of BEING versus HAVING."

Abundance and Being

I think Hopkins' series of questions is brilliant because it forces us to reconsider what is really and truly important in our lives. I see so many people in our world obsessing about *having*, and I feel sorry for them. People who make *having* their end goal will never be happy because they'll never *have* everything they desire, no matter how rich they become. People are positioning themselves for failure when they make most of their goals based on *having* more.

On the other hand, people who establish goals based on *being* — as opposed to having — can find fulfillment in life. If your goals are to

BE a better parent, or to BE a better spouse, or to BE a better neighbor, then you're positioning yourself for success, because all of these goals are achievable and genuinely fulfilling, wouldn't you agree?

True wisdom means understanding that the abundant life is found in the realm of being, not in the realm of having. The world may offer a life of abundance, but what we're all truly seeking is an abundant life — and there's a big difference between the two!

When we position ourselves in life in terms of acquiring the riches of the world, we're *positioning ourselves for having*. But when we position ourselves in terms of riches of relationships, we are *positioning ourselves for being*. One does not, by necessity, preclude the other. In fact, *goals for having can complement goals for being* when people understand that money is a means to an end, not an end in itself.

POSITIONING OUR LIVES IN RELATION TO TIME

Sociologists maintain that our primary shaping comes from our environment. Geneticists maintain that our future is dependent upon the characteristics we inherit from our biological parents. However, both would agree that the *choices* we make shape our lives in dramatic fashion, particularly in the way in which we position ourselves to time.

We cannot experience the abundant life in the here and now if we are living in the past. As a wise person once said, "Yesterday is a cancelled check. Tomorrow is a promissory note. Today is the only cash you have. Spend it wisely." The individual who lives in the past does a grave injustice to himself, for he wastes the present and doesn't allow for the future.

Escape from the Past

Oprah Winfrey is one individual who refused to allow herself to become trapped in her past. Sociologists and geneticists alike would normally predict that there was little hope for her, but she believed in herself and knew that she could become somebody important.

Oprah's past had certainly given her a plethora of excuses to fail. Raised in poverty, Oprah was raped, molested, abused, and rejected as a child. Yet despite all these horrible experiences in her formative years, and against all the odds, she became a success. How? By setting goals that would help her BE a better person and by choosing to let go of her past, rather than choosing to remain chained to it.

Oprah went on to graduate from high school and college, and worked as a newscaster at a small TV station in the South. She washed out as a newscaster, but she excelled in interviewing people, so she capitalized on her interviewing talent to eventually become the host of the most popular daytime program on TV. She even ventured into acting, winning an Oscar nomination for her screen debut in the movie, *The Color Purple.*

Oprah became a success despite her background because she positioned herself for success, pure and simple. The lesson to be learned is simple also: If she can move beyond her past, so can you. If she can achieve goals for becoming a better person, so can you.

Time Is Your Most Precious Commodity

What would you do if you had a bank account that was credited with $84,600 at the beginning of each day, but which would not allow you to carry your unused balance from one day to the next? Unless you like to throw money away, you'd draw out every single cent before the end of the day, isn't that true?

Well, each of us has just such a "bank account" called *time.* Each day 84,600 seconds are deposited into our account, and if we don't use the time wisely, then we lose it. Ben Franklin summed it up this way:

> *Dost thou love life?*
> *Then do not squander time,*
> *for that is the stuff life is made of.*

Franklin understood the dangers of positioning ourselves in the past, for then we are unable to enjoy the present. And when we're unable to live in the present, we're unable to be set free from the shackles of our past. Hence, only those who position themselves in the present and the future can experience the abundant life.

As a friend of mine always says, "Live for today and plan for tomorrow." I couldn't agree more.

POSITIONING OUR LIVES IN RELATION TO OTHERS

I'm continually amazed when I read about actors and entertainers who destroy themselves with drinking or drugs or who commit suicide when they perceive their popularity is waning. Elvis Presley and Marilyn Monroe come to mind right away, of course.

Their mistake was to position themselves inappropriately in regard to others. People who define their self-worth by seeking public approval are just setting themselves up for a big hurt because they're seeking to *receive love* from others, rather than to *give love* to others.

We can't enjoy the rewards of the abundant life when we seek to receive love from strangers because it's based on falsehoods. When an actor acts and movie-goers adore him for his acting, what they're really saying is "We love you for your act, not for you." And at some level, every performer with his feet on the ground understands that the love they receive from audiences is temporary and conditional — and they treat it accordingly.

That's the difference between the Elvis Presley's of the entertainment world and the Jimmy Stewart's. Elvis deceived himself into believing the adoration was real and that he needed it to feel good about himself. But no matter how much attention he received, it was never enough. He died of a drug overdose at the age of 42.

Jimmy Stewart, on the other hand, understood the "love" he received from his fans for what it was — conditional and fleeting. Because he had his feet squarely on the ground, he was able to separate his public life from his private life. As a result, he was able to commit himself to his loving wife of 40-plus years, and he enjoyed an adoring circle of family and friends. By all accounts, he gave as much love to them as he got. He died at peace with himself at the ripe old age of 82.

Tom Brokaw's Humbling Experience

I remember hearing Tom Brokaw tell a story that helped him put his celebrity status in the right perspective. Brokaw had recently been promoted to host of *The Today Show*, and he was feeling quite proud of his accomplishment.

After all, he had begun in Omaha, Nebraska, then progressed to Los Angeles and later to Washington, D.C., before finally making it to the top in the Big Apple. He'd come a long way and was feeling a bit full of himself.

One day as he was walking around Bloomingdale's in New York City, Brokaw had a feeling he was being watched. Out of the corner of his eye he spied a man peeking at him through the tie racks. Brokaw thought to himself how wonderful it was to be recognized as a celebrity. Finally, the man got up the courage to approach Brokaw.

"You're Tom Brokaw, aren't you?"

"Yes," Brokaw replied.

"You used to be on the morning news on KMTV in Omaha, right?" the man continued.

"That's right," said Brokaw, thinking to himself that the man would soon be congratulating him on how far he had come in a few short years.

"I knew it the minute I saw you," the man beamed. "Say, whatever happened to you?"

Brokaw laughs when he tells that story, and he says that during times when he's feeling full of self-importance, he reminds himself of that incident. Brokaw has his feet on the ground because he understands that when we position ourselves in places of importance, we are inevitably setting ourselves up for a fall. We have also lost focus on what is truly important in life.

Higher, Orville, Higher

Bishop Milton Wright was a person who probably wouldn't be remembered were it not for his two famous sons, Orville and Wilbur Wright. As you will recall from grade school, the Wright brothers were the first men to build and fly an airplane.

In 1910 Bishop Wright, at the age of 81, flew over a prairie in Ohio in a plane piloted by his two sons. Orville was concerned that the flight might unnerve his father, but his concern was ill-founded. For not long after the plane had taken off, Orville could hear his father shout above the roar of the engines, *"Higher, Orville, higher!"*

Bishop Wright's declaration should be the clarion call for the flight of our own lives, no matter what our station in life. Only by seeking lofty goals that will help us BE more can we ever hope to achieve the abundance that we deserve.

The abundant life calls us to position ourselves on a higher plane than selfishness or pride. It calls us to serve. Our accomplishments, achievements, and acquisitions mean nothing if we have no one to share them with. And they shouldn't be used to elevate ourselves above others but to place us in proper relationship to them.

It is only when we nurture and cultivate the higher qualities of life — such as love and joy and peace — that we can begin to participate fully in the abundant life. John Wesley said it best when he wrote this directive on how to live a life of abundance:

"Do all the good you can/

74

in all the ways you can/
in all the places you can/
at all the times you can/
to all the people you can/
as long as ever you can."

Serving Is an Attitude, Not a Position

Many years ago a young minister was interviewed by a church newspaper as to why he had joined the ministry. He responded that he felt called to serve his neighbor and his God.

The newspaper received many letters during the following weeks inquiring as to why the young man felt he could only serve God in the ministry. The authors of the letters said they, too, loved God, and they served God mightily through their vocations.

And, of course, they were right. This anecdote reveals to us the notion that it's not the profession that determines our relationship to God and our neighbors, but rather *how we position ourselves* in those relationships. Consequently, in whatever we do in life, the difference between *having* and *being* is the difference between whether we position ourselves to serve others — or we position others so that others serve us.

Genuine relationships with others are always two-way streets in which we learn to cultivate the relationship by learning to both give and receive.

REVIEW

The abundant life is found when you position your life in relationship to your goals and objectives, to your time, and to your neighbor.

Positioning our lives in relation to our goals

When we position ourselves in terms of acquiring riches, we're positioning ourselves *to have more.* When we position ourselves in terms of enriching our relationships, we're positioning ourselves *to be more.* Therefore, working toward goals that help us BE MORE instead of HAVE MORE will result in our living a life of true abundance.

Positioning our lives in relation to time

Ben Franklin understood the importance of time when he said, *"Dost thou love life? Then do not squander time, for that is the stuff that life is made of."* The key to abundance is "living for today and planning for tomorrow."

Positioning our lives in relation to others

When we seek to receive love, as opposed to give love, in order to increase our self worth, we are setting ourselves up for a big fall. Only by positioning ourselves to nurture the higher qualities of life — love, joy, and peace — can we begin to fully participate in the abundant life.

CHAPTER 6

∿

CHOOSING YOUR DESTINY

*I find the great thing in this world is not so much
where we stand, as in what direction we are moving: To reach the port of heaven, we must sail sometimes with the wind and sometimes against it —
but we must sail, and not drift, nor be at anchor.*
— Oliver Wendell Holmes

Bill had not been feeling well for quite some time,
so his wife made an appointment for him to see a doctor. After
examining Bill, the doctor told him that he wanted to speak to his
wife, Susan, while Bill was getting dressed.

The doctor took Susan into his office and explained that Bill had
a rare and potentially fatal, stress-related disease. If Bill were to
survive, she would have to radically change her life-style so that
she could attend to his needs. The doctor explained in detail what

Susan had to do.

First of all, she would have to give up her successful career to stay home and take care of Bill. She would need to get up an hour before him each day, shower and get dressed, and provide a stress-free environment for him.

She would need to supervise his diet and provide him with fresh fruit and grains for breakfast, fruit and greens for lunch, and a home-cooked meal for dinner every night. During the day, while Bill was at work, she would have to clean the house from top to bottom to eliminate allergic and pathogenic sources of stress.

When Bill came home from work, she needed to meet him at the door with a big smile, a hug, and a kiss. And during the evening, she would have to serve his every whim to make sure he was re-laxed before going to bed. In effect, she had to become Bill's slave.

"Are all these changes absolutely necessary?" Susan inquired.

"Yes," the physician responded. "If these changes don't occur starting today, then Bill will surely die."

"What did the doctor say?" Bill asked Susan on the way home from the doctor's office.

After a few moments of deep thought, Susan answered som-berly, *"Honey, he said you're going to die."*

Life Is Made up of Choices

The story reminds us, in a very humorous fashion, that the choices we make in life can have a profound impact on ourselves and those around us. Fortunately, unlike Susan, most of our choices don't in-volve life-and-death decisions. But when we add our choices up, they make the difference between living a life of abundance and living a life of poverty.

As I see it, one of the great problems in America today is an unwill-ingness for some people to take responsibility for the poor choices they have made.

For example, if we spill hot coffee on ourselves, we sue McDonald's. If we smoke two packs of cigarettes a day and get cancer, we sue the tobacco industry. And if we murder someone's child and the parents testify against us in court, then we sue them for slander — which is exactly what happened according to a recent episode of *60 Minutes*. The sad thing is, all too often these irresponsible "victims" win their cases.

Making the Right Choices

In every decision we make, we're confronted with a choice. We don't have the option of avoiding making choices because a decision to do nothing is, in fact, a choice!

Bad choices can loom over us for extended periods, and sometimes they can even lead to our ruin. Good choices, on the other hand, can result in positive consequences that enable us to experience the abundant life. Each day of our lives we find ourselves at the crossroads of hundreds of decisions, and each of those decisions will ultimately determine the way in which we experience life.

So how do we go about making the right choices? In the rest of this chapter you'll discover seven fundamental principles that will guide you to making consistently wise choices that will lead to a life of abundance.

CHOOSING THE HARD WAY OVER THE EASY WAY

We make the right choices when we are willing to take the hard way over the easy way. We live in a world of fast computers, fast cars, fast food, fast this, and fast that. As a consequence, we have the tendency to try to do everything in as short a time span as possible.

This often means that we take the *easy way* as opposed to the *right way*. Unfortunately, Ben Franklin's observation that "Haste makes waste" rings as true today as it did 200 years ago, and all too often we find that the quick "gain" ends up hurting us in the long run.

Too Busy to Live?

I'd like to tell you a story about a woman named Jennifer Johnson because it illustrates how we can literally rush ourselves into death when we choose the fast, easy way over the slow, hard way.

My story begins with an angry, frightened Jennifer Johnson banging her hands on the steering wheel of her car. She'd been in such a rush all day that she kept ignoring the fact that her car was nearly out of gas. She'd passed a dozen gas stations in the course of her day, but she kept choosing to wait for a more convenient time to fill up.

Now it was too late. Her car was out of gas, it was dark outside, and Jennifer was sitting in a section of town that had been torn by riots just weeks earlier.

As she reached to lock her car doors, she quickly surveyed the dimly lit streets, looking for a pay phone, a service station, a restaurant — anything! But the streets were barren. Jennifer had not prayed in years, but now she began to pray that a police car or taxi would come to her assistance.

Suddenly, she noticed to her horror that a man was walking down the middle of the street heading straight for her car. She slid down into her seat, hoping that he would pass by. When she looked up, he was staring at her through the passenger window. She became hysterical and cried out, "Get away. Leave me alone. Don't bother me." He began tapping on the window. He was saying something, but in her panicked state, she couldn't understand the words.

The man ran around the car, trying to pull open each door, but they were all locked. Jennifer began to flash her lights and blow her horn to drive him away, and finally he disappeared into the darkness. She was relieved, but only for a moment, for she could see the man re-emerging from the shadows carrying a six-foot-long piece of two-by-four lumber. He tried to speak to her again, but she still couldn't make out what he was saying. Suddenly, he swung the board at the passenger's window. Shattered glass sprayed into Jennifer's face and lap.

Pulled out of the Car

The man unlocked the passenger door, opened it, and reached in to grab her, but she slid to the far side of the car and began kicking at him. Soon his face was bloodied from her kicks, but he managed to grab onto her legs and drag her onto the pavement.

She fought and kicked him as he carried her 40 feet down the deserted street. Then he lowered her gently to the pavement, saying, "Don't be afraid. I'm not going to hurt you."

Jennifer crawled to a nearby fence and pulled herself up, preparing to fight her attacker to the death, if necessary. Then she heard a low rumble ... the ground began to shake ... lights began to flash ... and she looked over to see a train smash right into the side of her car!

At that moment Jennifer realized that the man was not trying to hurt her. Her car had stopped on the train tracks, and the stranger was only trying to save her from the speeding train.

Different Choices, Different Consequences

How different the day could have been if Jennifer had not taken what she thought was the easy way out, but instead had taken a little time and gone a little out of her way to fill her car with gas. What profound consequences that simple choice had. Jennifer, by the way, still wakes up in the middle of the night, horrified at what could have happened.

Like Jennifer, all of us have driven by a convenient gas station when we should have pulled in for a fill-up, and then suffered the consequences of having to walk to the nearest service station. We learn the hard way that there is great truth in the old adage, "Do not put off until tomorrow what you can do today."

Sure, it's easier to postpone doing the little things than to stop and deal with them right now, but how many times do the long-term consequences turn out to be far worse than the temporary inconvenience? And in Jennifer's case, the consequences could have been fatal!

I tell you this story to point out that not every wall in our lives seems like a big wall at the time. In fact, our days are mostly littered with little walls that we have to jump over or walk around. But the story of Jennifer reminds us that our choices determine our fate, so we need to choose carefully.

CHOOSING THE LONG WAY OVER THE SHORT WAY

We make the right choices when we're willing to take the long way over the short way. This doesn't mean that the long way is always the best way. But it does mean that we should consider both ways before we act, and if the long way is the right way, we have to be willing to take it.

When Henry Kissinger was Secretary of State, he often asked his staff to prepare written recommendations on the major political issues. When he received these reports, he would table them for 48 hours, and then hand them back to his staff with the question, "Is this the best you can do?"

Invariably they would respond, "Well, no sir, there may be some ways that we could improve the report. Perhaps we could document it better, and we could probably predict some outcomes in the event our recommendations aren't followed." Then Kissinger would ask the staff member to revise his report and submit it again later.

The staff would go over the report line by line, rewriting the sections that they found lacking. When they submitted the revised report, once again Kissinger would table it for a few days before asking, "Is this the best you can do?"

More often than not the staff member would stare at his feet and mumble something like, "Well, perhaps the language could be tightened a bit, and some of the data could be updated." Kissinger would hand the report back to the staff member, requesting yet another revision within the week.

Kissinger and his staff would go through this routine three or four more times before the staff could look Kissinger squarely in the eye and say, "This is the best we can do. We have reviewed every detail and believe you can present it to the President in full confidence."

It was only at this point that Kissinger would even bother to read the document. You see, Kissinger made the right decisions more often than not because he didn't take the shortcuts in life — and he didn't allow the people around him to take shortcuts, either.

The Shortest Way Can Take the Longest Time

When I was attending seminary in Atlanta, I was active with youth groups at a small church I was attending. Many of my charges had never been skiing, so I took great delight in organizing ski trips, which were relatively inexpensive because I worked out arrangements with youth directors of local churches that had much better facilities than ours.

I remember one trip that proves that shortcuts can easily turn into "longcuts." We had originally planned to travel to a ski site by way of an interstate highway. Just before departure, the youth director looked at the map and noticed that the interstate wasn't the most direct route to the ski area. He calculated that he could shave off 100 miles or more by taking the state highways.

What the director didn't take into account is that in South Carolina, North Carolina, and Tennessee, many of the back roads are closed or slow moving during heavy snowfalls. Only the interstates are open for travel when the snow is heavy. Sure enough, the backroads were clogged with snow, while the interstate was clear. As a result, the "shortcut" saved 100 miles, but it added eight hours of travel time!

This story reminds us that appearances can be deceiving, and that the shortest distance between two points is NOT always a straight line. Have you ever noticed how mountain roads seldom go straight up the mountain, but rather zig-zag back and forth across the hillside until they reach the top? Likewise, sometimes we need to climb the walls in our lives in a zig-zag pattern because the short way isn't always faster than the long way.

CHOOSING THE DISCIPLINED WAY OVER THE UNDISCIPLINED WAY

Hurricane Andrew will long be remembered for the tremendous destruction it left behind when it hit land just south of Miami in 1992. Several months later, CNN sent in a news crew to report on the re-building process.

The news footage showed homes at various stages of reconstruction. Some frustrated homeowners complained on camera that their insurance companies had been insensitive to their needs. Others complained that the government red tape had kept them from getting their building permits, severely delaying their rebuilding plans.

Interestingly enough, as the news crew made its way down a hard-hit street, they came to a house that was in perfect condition. The owner was even in the front yard mowing the grass. The reporters inquired as to how long it took him to rebuild. He responded that he didn't have to rebuild, for the hurricane had caused only minor damage to his home.

Following the Rules

The reporters looked dumbfounded. They asked how his house could have escaped damage when hundreds of houses all around him were flattened.

"When I built my house," he explained, "I just followed the Florida building code. If the code said use two-by-six lumber, I used a two-by-six. If it said to use a certain size nail, I used that nail. I did just what the code said to do. The building inspectors told me before I started building that if I followed the code, my house would withstand a hurricane. They were right. I guess no one else around here followed the code."

He was right. Government authorities attributed much of the damage to poorly constructed homes that didn't conform to the building codes.

We learn from this story that we make the right decisions when we're willing to choose the disciplined way, as opposed to the un-disciplined way. Discipline literally brings order out of chaos. As we become more disciplined in life, we find that we become more productive, and as we become more productive, we're often able to achieve the impossible. Quite often our productivity increases when we discipline ourselves to keep our eyes on the goal and not the distractions along the way.

Don't Major in the Minor Things

We make the right choices when we're disciplined and don't allow our focus to shift from the goal to the walls in front of it. I learned this lesson firsthand when I attended Vanderbilt University in Nashville, Tennessee, to finish my doctoral studies.

My wife went to work for Coca-Cola in Raleigh, North Carolina, which was more than 200 miles from Nashville. We'd been married for less than a year, and my parents felt bad that we'd have to live apart during my schooling. I told them that we'd have the chance to see each other a couple of weekends a month, and that we were convinced this was the right thing to do. Furthermore, I felt there was an advantage to the separation because it meant I could devote my total energies to my studies and meet the rigorous deadline for graduation that I'd set for myself.

Graduating in Record Time

When I had first talked with the admissions office, they told me my time line for graduation was doable. But when I arrived at Vanderbilt, they changed their story a bit. They told me it was possible for me to make my graduation date, but it wasn't probable because it had never been done before.

One of the main obstacles to graduation was my doctoral dissertation, which usually took a year to get approved and then took another year or two to write. I was determined to graduate early, however, and I chose the dean of the divinity school at Vanderbilt as my advisor. I figured if anyone could help me make it happen, he could.

I attended my classes during the day and worked into the early hours of the morning on my doctoral proposal, my final dissertation, and my studies. During spring break I had the opportunity to vacation with my wife, but I turned it down, choosing instead to concentrate on my studies. It was a tough choice, but, I felt, a very necessary one.

Meeting My Deadline

I'm proud to say that I was able to meet my original deadline. The dean said after graduation that he didn't know how I did it! That is the power of determination and discipline. I certainly wasn't the smartest student in the program, but discipline enabled me to accomplish my goals.

You see, I had a goal, and I was determined to climb every wall and build every door necessary to accomplish my goal. I'm living proof that by choosing the disciplined way you can accomplish things that no one has accomplished before.

The disciplined life-style can enable great things to happen. An undisciplined life-style can have just the opposite effect. Several years ago I remember reading that there are four ways to elude success:

1. Don't look.
2. Don't listen.
3. Don't think.
4. Don't make decisions — they may be right.

These same four rules also contain the key to achieving success. All you have to do is break all four rules, and you're automatically on the road to success, no matter what the task!

CHOOSING THE THOUGHTFUL WAY OVER THE THOUGHTLESS WAY

We make the right choices when we're willing to choose the thoughtful way over the thoughtless way. People wouldn't ever choose the easy, the short, or the undisciplined way if they had taken the time to really THINK about it. We make the right choices in our lives when we prepare our hearts, minds, and souls for the challenges that life will bring.

General Patton's Philosophy

General George S. Patton will long be remembered as a brilliant military strategist. His philosophy in battle is applicable to all of life.

He said, "Now if you're going to win any battle, you have to do one thing. You have to make the mind run the body. Never let the body tell the mind what to do. The body will always give up. The body is always tired, morning, noon, and night. But the body is never tired if the mind is not tired. When you were younger, the mind could make you dance all night, and the body was never tired ... You've always got to make the mind take over and keep going."

George Patton knew that the mind is what prepares us for life's battles, both literally and figuratively. When our minds are prepared appropriately, we're setting the stage to receive handsome dividends.

Patton understood that preparation wasn't something you did once and then never had to do again, like graduating from high school. He understood that preparation was a lifelong process.

A sign above a retired army officer's desk says it best: "Before you decide about your aim, check your ammunition." It's the same in life as it is in battle. You don't check your ammunition once and then never check it again as long as you live. You check your ammunition before each and every battle so that you have the best chance for survival.

Wood-Chopping Contest

It's like the story about the cocky, young lumberjack who challenged the local champion to an all-day wood-chopping contest.

The challenger worked very hard, stopping only for a brief lunch break. The champion enjoyed a leisurely lunch, and took several long breaks during the day.

At the end of the day the challenger was surprised and annoyed to discover that the champion had chopped substantially more wood than he had.

"I don't get it," the challenger said scratching his head. "Every time I looked over your way, you were taking a rest, yet you chopped more wood than I did."

"But what you didn't notice," said the winning woodsman, "was that when I sat down to rest, I was sharpening my ax."

This anecdote paints a vivid picture of the importance of choosing to commit ourselves to lifelong preparation. If we don't stop and sharpen our skills from time to time, we'll end up working harder while being less productive — especially in today's competitive environment.

We're living in the information age, and the battle between brains and brawn is over — and brains won going away. That's why today, more than ever, we need to prepare ourselves for success by choosing the thoughtful way over the thoughtless way in life.

CHOOSING UNITY OVER SEPARATION

We make the right decisions when we choose not to go it alone, but rather to seek to be united with others in achieving goals, aims, and aspirations in life.

It should be noted, however, that there is a vast difference between union and unity. A pair of handcuffs may bring *union* between a criminal and a law enforcement officer, but it most certainly doesn't bring unity.

Union implies that we're together in time and place, but *unity* implies we're together in mind and spirit. Union implies we're together in location, but unity means we're working together. Union isn't necessarily bad, but if we're sincere about climbing walls and opening doors in our lives, we need to possess a common spirit of unity.

As the Bible notes, *"A house divided cannot stand."* It's no coincidence that Abraham Lincoln evoked this very same Biblical passage time and again when asked to justify his decision to fight the Civil War rather than allow the South to split from the Union.

Why Unity Is Crucial to Survival

A scientist at UCLA studied groups of individuals who were cut off from society in an effort to determine what led to the demise of some groups and the survival of others. The results of the study revealed that the vital factor for survival was a unifying force that rallied the individuals together.

Among the groups that survived was a group of Japanese soldiers who hid on the island of Guam, and other Pacific Islands, for more than 30 years after World War II. Long after the war ended, the soldiers posted sentries, mended nets, and set bonfires for Japanese rescue vessels that never came. They were able to survive because they were united by their common desire to win the war, and they rallied together in support of a common cause that was larger than each individual person.

A well-known group that didn't survive was the crew of the British naval ship, *The HMS Bounty*, made famous in the book and movie, *Mutiny on the Bounty*. In 1789, after enjoying three peaceful months in idyllic Tahiti, the crew refused to sail back to England.

The crew banded together and took over the ship, setting the captain and officers afloat in a raft. Then the mutineers sailed back to Tahiti, where they kidnapped a small group of Tahitian men and women for slaves, and they headed off to live on a nearby island.

Eighteen years later, an American whaling vessel landed on the island and discovered that only one of the original crew members was still alive. Their constant quarrels, arguments, and fights over the women led to murder and suicide.

Because they lacked unity, they had nothing to rally around except their own self-serving lusts, which inevitably led to their division and demise.

The Great Wall of China

The Great Wall of China is yet another example that union is essential for our survival. Just prior to the construction of the Great Wall, China was a feudal society made up of scores of separate, warring empires.

The leader of the biggest city-state in China, Emperor Qin, built the wall in sections to protect his lands from Mogul invaders from the north. The wall served its purpose, and it helped Emperor Qin to pull most of the warring factions into one great empire.

The Great Wall of China brought temporary *union* to the people of China, but it couldn't bring *unity*, for the internal power struggles once again tore ancient China apart. You see, the Great Wall could help fend off outside invaders, but not the "invaders" from within, proving once again that "a house divided cannot stand."

These examples serve to remind us that we make the right choices in life when we unite with others in the attainment of common goals, dreams, visions, and aspirations.

CHOOSING PEOPLE OVER THINGS

Sometimes we make the mistake of seeking fulfillment in life by surrounding ourselves with an *abundance of things*, as opposed to an *abundance of relationships*. Although many humans have sought their security in worldly riches, the most important things in life can't be purchased. After all, what good are our riches if we don't have anyone to share them with?

Money Madness

In the early 1980s, the trial of Claus von Bulow made all the headlines. As you will recall, von Bulow was the Newport, Rhode Island, aristocrat who was accused of attempting to murder his wife, Martha von Bulow, with insulin injections. An article in the January 22, 1982, edition of the *San Francisco Chronicle* carried this summary comment:

"The characters in this story — Sunny, Claus, and their friends — don't worry much about how to make the world nicer for others; they worry mainly about how to preserve every cent they have inherited, how to increase their fortunes, and how to have as much pleasure as possible. The trouble is, in the end, none of it seems to have given them much pleasure."

The tragic story of the von Bulow's is not unlike Charles Dickens' classic story, *The Christmas Carol*. Of course, the one major difference is that Dickens' story ends happily, as Scrooge discovers that there is more to life than the accumulation of wealth. The point is simple, yet profound: Our possessions can become dangerous when we put them ahead of people.

Don't Drown in Greed

It's like the story of the passenger on a sinking ship who didn't want to lose all of his gold, which was stored on board. So he fastened a belt containing 200 pounds of gold around himself and jumped overboard. Later he was found anchored to the bottom with the gold still strapped to his body. The question he must have asked himself as he was gasping his last breath was, "Do I have the gold ... or does the gold have me?"

Rudyard Kipling, the great English writer, delivered a commencement address at McGill University in Montreal, Canada. In his speech Kipling drove home the danger of viewing money or position as an end in and of itself.

He said, "Some day you will meet a man who cares for none of these things. Then you will know how poor you are." Kipling was well aware of the danger of seeing one's possessions as an end in themselves, and not the means to an end.

CHOOSING A CENTERED LIFE-STYLE

There is one more thing that we must take into account if we want our choices to be on target. Our lives must be appropriately centered or else the choices we make can miss the mark.

George Bush tells a moving story about the importance of centering our lives on something larger and more permanent than the vagaries of this world.

When Bush was President of the United States, he attended the funeral of Soviet leader Brezhnev. The funeral, though run with military precision, was a cold and hollow occasion, as soldiers marched with gleaming bayonets, and the state-run media used the occasion to proclaim the usual Marxist propaganda.

There were no prayers at the funeral or comforting hymns — and no mention of God. The Soviet leaders took their places along the Kremlin wall as the family silently escorted the casket to its final resting place.

"I happened to be in just the right spot to see Mrs. Brezhnev," Bush noted later. "She walked up, took a last look at her husband, and there, in the cold grey center of that atheist state, she traced the sign of the cross over her husband's chest.

"I was stunned, and I was deeply moved," Bush continued. "Anyone who witnessed that loving gesture could not accept any moral foundation for communism. It became clear to me. Decades, even centuries of harsh, secular rule can never destroy the spark of true faith."

The Center That Endures

Brezhnev had taken the hard, the long, the difficult, and the thoughtful way, but he erred when he placed his faith in communism instead of God. As a result, his life wasn't appropriately centered, for what he had centered his faith around is now gone. Mrs. Brezhnev, on the other hand, centered her faith around something that will endure for eternity — God.

Faith in communism has waned in Russia today, but faith in God continues to grow, even though decades of communism had sought to extinguish it. Likewise, the greatness of America lies in our faith in God, a faith expressed in the cornerstones of our nation, from our Constitution ... to our Bill of Rights ... to our currency.

And so it is, "In God We Trust."

REVIEW

In every decision we make, we're confronted with a choice. We don't have the option of avoiding the decision-making process because, in essence, even when we choose to do nothing, we're still making a choice.

Bad choices can loom over us for extended periods, and sometimes they can even lead to our ruin. Good choices can result in positive benefits and consequences and enable us to experience the abundant life. There are seven principles that guide us to making the right choices:

Principle 1: Choose the hard way over the easy way

We live in a world of fast computers, fast cars, and fast food. As a consequence, we have a tendency to try to do everything in as short a time span as possible. This often means that we take the easy way as opposed to the right way.

Principle 2: Choose the long way over the short way

We make the right choices when we're willing to take the long way over the short way. This doesn't mean that the long way is always the best way, but it does mean that we should consider both ways before we act. Ironically, sometimes the shortest distance between two points is NOT a straight line.

Principle 3: Choose the disciplined way over the undisciplined way

As we become more disciplined in life, we find that we become more productive. And as we become more productive, we're often able to achieve what we, and perhaps others also, previously considered to be impossible.

Principle 4: Choose the thoughtful way over the thoughtless way

No one would ever choose the easy, the short, or the undisciplined way if they had taken the time to really *think* about it. The right choices are made in our life when we prepare our hearts, minds, and souls for the challenges that life will bring.

Principle 5: Choose unity over separation

There's a big difference between union and unity. A pair of hand-cuffs may bring *union* between a police officer and a criminal, but it certainly won't bring about unity. A common spirit of *unity* is essential because "a house divided cannot stand."

Principle 6: Choose people over things

Sometimes we begin to seek fulfillment by seeking a life of abundant things, as opposed to a life of abundant relationships. Although many have sought security in worldly riches, the most important things in life can't be purchased. After all, what good are our riches if we don't have anyone to share them with?

Principle 7: Choose an appropriately centered life-style

We make the right choices in life when we're willing to take the hard, the long, the difficult, the thoughtful, the united, and the people-oriented way in life ... and when that way is centered in one greater than ourselves — eternal and not temporal in nature — our God. It is then that we know that our decisions will be lasting and true.

CHAPTER 7

—

LEARNING WHEN TO BE QUICK AND SLOW

For all your days prepare,
And meet them ever alike;
When you are the anvil, bear —
When you are the hammer, strike.
— Edwin Markham

An old country preacher spent a great deal of time in preparing his weekly sermons, and he was especially pleased with his latest effort.

When Sunday arrived he drove out to his church in the country, only to discover that only one parishioner showed up for the morning service. The minister debated what he should do. Should he deliver the whole sermon? Just part of it? Or should he call off the service entirely?

The minister decided that because this one parishioner was committed enough to show up each Sunday, and because the minister had worked so faithfully on the message for that day, he would deliver the entire sermon. And so he did.

At the end of the service, he walked to the back of the sanctuary to shake hands with the lone parishioner. The minister asked the parishioner what he thought of his sermon.

The parishioner thought for a moment and then responded, "Preacher, I want you to know something. I'm a farmer, and every day I fill my wagon and take hay down to my cows to eat at the trough during feeding time. But when I go down to the trough at feeding time, and there is only one cow there, I don't drop the whole load."

A Short Prescription for Personal Conduct

This story teaches us that different situations call for different responses. A sincere heart-to-heart conversation between the minister and the parishioner would have been more appropriate to the occasion than a full-blown sermon, wouldn't you agree?

This story reminds us that it's necessary for us to live our lives according to certain rules. But when it's all said and done, it's better to follow the spirit of the law than the letter of the law.

The Bible spells out three key principles that we should take to heart, for these principles should inform and guide our conduct in virtually every situation:

"Everyone should be quick to listen, slow to speak, and slow to anger."

Isn't that an amazingly powerful statement? One simple sentence tells us virtually everything we need to know about how we should conduct ourselves in the presence of others.

Let's take a look at each of these principles in a little more depth so that we fully understand the wisdom contained in this short verse.

QUICK TO LISTEN

The first great principle that we learn is that we should be "quick to listen." I'd take it one step further and say we need to not only hear the words, we need to *listen to the message*. You see, there is more to listening than simply hearing. It's one thing to *hear* a message. It's another thing to truly *listen* to it ... to take the information contained in that message and put it to good use.

When we're quick to listen, it means we're eager to receive a person's message and we're open to applying it to our own lives. In other words, quick to listen is the opposite of "going in one ear and out the other."

I'd like to tell you a story about some young people who failed to heed this wisdom. They heard a message of warning, but tragically, they weren't "quick to listen."

Hiking in Bear Country

In 1967 five young people were hiking to a campsite in Montana's Glacier National Park. The young people were vivacious, funloving, and full of life, but, like many young people, they didn't like taking advice from adults — and they were convinced nothing bad could happen to them.

So they weren't "quick to listen" to the warnings of a group of campers who told the young backpackers that a grizzly bear had chased after them earlier in the day. The young campers headed deeper and deeper into the wilderness area, arriving at their campsite just as darkness fell. But the darker it got, the less brave the campers became, so they agreed to build a large fire to scare away any wild intruders.

As the campers were resting around the fire, they looked up through the smoke to see a huge grizzly lurking nearby. As the grizzly entered their campsite, the young campers slid quietly into their sleeping bags and lay motionless, praying the bear would go away.

The bear sniffed around one of the bags and then began to rip it open. The other four campers bolted into the woods, where they could hear 19-year-old Michelle Koons screaming as the bear dragged her away in her sleeping bag.

The next day the four survivors hiked back to a ranger station and reported the incident. Within days the rangers tracked down and shot the bear suspected in the attack. Upon closer inspection, the rangers identified human blood and flesh on the bear's paws. Michelle had been killed and partially devoured by the rogue grizzly.

This tragedy could have been averted if only the young people had been "quick to listen." They heard the words of other campers as they headed deeper into the woods, but their failure to really listen and respond accordingly ended in tragedy.

How often we could save ourselves a great deal of trouble if only we would listen to others, such as concerned friends and family, and respond appropriately.

Whispering Gallery

The dome of St. Paul's Cathedral features an amazing phenomenon called the "Whispering Gallery." By virtue of the dome's unique design, someone standing on one side of the dome can whisper a few words, and the sound will travel around the dome until it can be heard distinctly by someone on the other side.

This strange phenomenon can also be found occasionally in nature, and when an ancient tyrant named Dionysius heard about a whispering cavern in Syracuse, Italy, he used it to his advantage. The outside entrance to the cave was shaped like an ear, and in time, the cave became known as "the ear of Dionysius" — and for good reason.

High up in the cavern, concealed in the ceiling, is a chamber that can only be reached by a concealed path at the top. Anyone sitting in this hidden chamber can hear even the faintest whisper from the ground below.

The tyrant Dionysius would sit in the chamber and listen to the conversations among the slaves and prisoners working below him, thereby enabling him to uncover any plots to escape or to assassinate him. Dionysius knew the importance of "hearing quickly," and he used the cavern to his advantage.

Emerson said, "Every man is superior to me in some way and from him I can learn." When we are quick to listen, we can take advantage of Emerson's sage advice.

Hearing Does NOT Necessarily Equate with Believing

Listening quickly has a second dimension as well, for listening quickly doesn't necessarily mean we take everything we hear at face value. If you saw the movie *Forrest Gump*, you'll know just what I'm talking about. Because Forrest was mentally slow, he took people's words literally. If someone told Forrest to go jump in the lake, guess what — Forrest would head straight for a lake and jump right in.

Listening quickly doesn't imply that we're to become like Forrest and take every piece of advice given to us. But it does imply that we evaluate others' advice before deciding what course of action to take.

A great musician was once asked to critique a piece of work. After the first performance he responded, "One cannot critique a musical composition from one performance, and I do not plan to listen to this one a second time."

The musician knew that it was a waste of time to listen to some things because they just don't measure up. Listening quickly doesn't mean we must give equal time to all things. But it does mean that when we hear something of substance and significance, we take it to heart.

SLOW TO SPEAK

The second principle is that we should be "slow to speak." All too often when we say what is on the tip of our tongue, even when it is said with the best of intentions, it comes out wrong. That's what the adage "Think before you speak" is all about. The following story illustrates what I'm saying:

It's Not What You Say, But How You Say It

An ancient king once dreamed that all his teeth had fallen out. He was naturally concerned about his dream, so the next morning he sent for a soothsayer to interpret his dream for him.

The soothsayer listened to the king's dream, pondered it for a moment, and then delivered this pronouncement:

"Your Highness, the dream means that all your relatives will die and you will be left alone."

The king was furious at the soothsayer's interpretation, and he demanded the soothsayer remove himself from the palace at once. Then the king called for a second soothsayer. This soothsayer listened to the king's dream, pondered for a moment, and then proclaimed:

"Rejoice, O King! The dream means that you will live many more years. In fact, you will outlive all your relatives! LONG LIVE THE KING!"

This interpretation so pleased the king that he gave the interpreter a large purse of gold.

Essentially, the two soothsayers made the same prediction. But there was a big difference in HOW they delivered the message, wouldn't you agree? As a result, there was a big difference in how the message was received. The moral of the story is very clear: It's not WHAT you say, but HOW you say it that counts!

Ask Instead of Order

I'm always amazed at the number of people who make the walls in their lives even higher and harder to climb because of their failure to be "slow to speak."

If you were an employee, for example, what message would you rather hear? "Your report is late again. What's wrong with you? Get your reports in on time or you're history!" Or would you prefer hearing, "It was my understanding this report was due two days ago. What do you suggest we do to make sure that future reports are submitted on time?"

In the first scenario, the boss attacks the employee on a personal level and orders him to change his behavior. All that does is cause anger and resentment, and most likely, the employee will look for ways to sabotage the boss' efforts in the future.

In the second scenario, the boss makes the late report the issue and then seeks the employee's input as to how to avoid missing deadlines in the future. Same message, different delivery. And, I'm sure, a different response from the employee. The point is we must be slow to speak so that the message we send is well received instead of ill received.

Likewise, we must also be slow to speak so that the message we deliver isn't misunderstood. The following true story illustrates what can happen when an unclear message is misunderstood.

Marriage Madness

A number of years ago, couples in Puerto Rico were getting married in record numbers. It seemed like everyone everywhere was getting married — and getting married quickly.

Why? Because a popular radio broadcaster announced that after June, all "caza" would be prohibited. Now, the word *caza* means "hunting" in Spanish, but it sounds very much like the Spanish word *casar*, which means "marriage."

As a result, thousands of Puerto Ricans understood the announcement to mean that all marriages would be prohibited after June! The radio host spoke too quickly, and as a result, his unclear message caused a minor panic.

When we speak too quickly, our message can be ill-received, misunderstood, or it can just plain get us deeper and deeper into trouble.

The Preacher and the Profiteer

Jim Bakker, the fallen TV evangelist, was convicted of fraud and initially sentenced to 45 years in prison and a $500,000 fine. Many federal sentencing experts thought Bakker's sentence was excessive, especially when his crimes were compared to a contemporary of Bakker's, a Wall Street junk bond trader named Ivan Boesky, who was eventually convicted of stealing hundreds of millions through illegal insider trading.

Boesky was sentenced to only 18 months in prison, plus a $50 million fine, which was not that steep considering Boesky reportedly had millions more than that stashed away in overseas banks.

Bakker ended up serving more than five years in prison, and when he returned to civilian life, he was virtually penniless. Boesky, on the other hand, served a much shorter sentence, and when he left prison, he returned to a life of privilege.

One Man Was Slow to Speak

The difference between Boesky and Bakker was that Boesky kept quiet during his legal proceedings, whereas Bakker, even after a jury of his peers found him guilty, defiantly maintained his innocence and expressed no remorse for his deeds. Many experts believe that it was his words after the fact, and not simply his deeds, that led to his harsh sentence.

As a minister, Bakker should have been very familiar with the advice to be "slow to speak." Sadly, however, Bakker refused to heed that advice. He learned the hard way that "biting your tongue" is usually preferable to speaking quickly out of passion or anger.

SLOW TO ANGER

The final principle is that we should be "slow to anger." This doesn't mean that anger is always bad. Nor does it mean we should never express anger. But it does mean that we're in charge of our emotions, and it's up to us to control our anger, rather than having our anger control us.

Using Anger to Your Advantage

Anger can be a very dangerous emotion. When we become angry quickly, we run the risk of losing the very thing we are seeking. The example of David Cone, the New York Mets pitcher who lost a game because he was so busy arguing angrily with an umpire to notice two runners scoring, is a good example. Cone's goal was to win the game, but his misplaced anger caused just the opposite to happen!

There's a fictitious story about Sinbad the Sailor that shows how uncontrolled anger can have the opposite of its intended effect. Sinbad and his sailors landed on a deserted tropical island. The only inhabitants were a tribe of small apes, and the apes had no intention of sharing their island with a "tribe" of strange-looking invaders.

The sailors were hungry and thirsty, but as they explored the island, they were unable to find anything to eat or drink. Then one sailor spotted coconuts in the palm trees high above them. The sailors were ecstatic, for they knew the coconuts could satisfy both their hunger and their thirst.

Only one problem. The coconuts were at the top of 50-foot palm trees. To make matters worse, the hostile apes were huddled together at the top of the trees, screeching and hissing at the sailors below.

Sinbad knew the trees were impossible to climb. And even if one of the men succeeded in climbing to the top, the hostile apes would attack him with a vengeance. Sinbad was a clever leader, however, and he devised a plan to gather up the coconuts without climbing the trees.

Monkey See, Monkey Do

Sinbad instructed his men to pick up all the sticks and stones they could find. At the count of three, the men threw the sticks and stones at the apes. The plan worked to perfection. As Sinbad anticipated, the apes became angry and soon they were grabbing ripe coconuts from the trees and hurling them back at the delighted sailors.

Sinbad had outsmarted his rivals. He faked anger in order to provoke real anger in the apes, and they fell into his trap. Because the apes were quick to anger, they ended up helping the very enemy they so despised.

This story points out that all too often our anger works against us and in favor of our antagonists.

An Angry God

"Be slow to anger" doesn't forewarn us against anger. It warns us against becoming angry too quickly.

God became angry with Moses when He called for Moses to lead the Hebrews out of Egyptian bondage, and four times Moses came up with excuses for ignoring God's commandment.

In the New Testament, we read that Jesus became angry after witnessing the temple in Jerusalem being overrun by money changers and sellers. He finally decided to express his anger, and He charged into the temple, upsetting the merchants' tables and chasing them out of the holy site.

These two stories remind us that anger is not apart from the personality of God or the people of God, for that matter. But anger should be used in its rightful place and, therefore, should always be slow to come and slow to respond.

Righteous Anger

Most everyone has experienced righteous indignation over injustice or ill treatment of others. I remember an incident in my own life that triggered righteous anger on the part of both my wife and me. The incident occurred when we were returning home from our honeymoon in the Bahamas.

We were at the Eastern Express check-in counter in the Bahamas preparing to board our return flight when we noticed three upper-class Bahamian women cut in line in front of a working-class Bahamian woman.

As if that weren't enough, the employee working the express counter was allowing the upper-class Bahamians to purchase tickets at her counter, even though express lines weren't supposed to sell tickets.

I was enjoying the last few hours of a terrific vacation, so I wasn't paying much attention to what was going on around us. But my wife was, and she was livid with indignation.

"Are we going to let those upper-class Bahamians take advantage of that poor little lady?" she turned and asked me. "Do something!"

I leaned forward to the lady and asked, "Doesn't that make you angry that those other ladies cut in front of you?"

She looked at me nervously, "On, no sir, it's all right."

I knew what she was *really* saying. There is a strong class structure in the Bahamas, and she was saying, "I know my place." That infuriated me, and I walked up to the employee working the counter and said, "These three women broke in line, and I don't appreciate your serving them."

The employee acted astonished and said, "I can't keep track of who is waiting in line and who is not."

"Well, I can," I responded, "and I'm telling you that these three women cut in front of this woman, and I want them to wait their turn."

About that time the American behind me said to the clerk, "I saw them break in line, too. I want your name, lady, so that I can write my friend, who is vice-president of Eastern. He needs to know about you. Everyone should wait their turn in line."

The rest of the passengers in line started to pitch in, and soon there was quite a commotion at our gate. It wasn't long before the upper-class Bahamians found themselves at the end of the line.

The little lady in front of us smiled and said, "thank you," because someone had cared enough to stand up and say that this woman was just as important as anyone else.

Stand Up and Be Counted

As children of God we must take a stand for *all* God's children, and in doing so, we have a right — make that an obligation — to express anger and outrage in the face of injustice.

I'll never forget Pastor Martin Niehmoller's declaration of guilt following World War II. He was ashamed that he and other church leaders failed to take a stand against the injustices perpetrated by the Nazis against millions of innocent people. In the end, everyone who remained silent paid a dear price for their neutrality. He wrote:

> They came for the Jews,
>> but since I was not a Jew, I said nothing;
> They came for the Catholics,
>> but since I was not a Catholic, I said nothing;
> They came for the trade unionists,
>> but since I was not a trade unionist, I said nothing;
> They came for the communists,
>> but since I was not a communist, I said nothing;
> And then they came for me
>> but now there was no one to say anything for anyone.

Because of their failure to rise in righteous indignation against the abuses of the government in the years leading up to WWII, the Christian Church in Germany failed to turn the tide of the Nazi movement before it was too late.

We live in a great nation, but unless we are willing to rise to the occasion in defense of our neighbor, we, too, can hand over our nation to the powers of evil and sin in the world.

We don't exist in a vacuum, and, as a result, we don't climb walls and open doors by ourselves. We need the cooperation of others if we're serious about accomplishing our goals in life, and the best way to get their cooperation is to be "quick to listen, slow to speak, and slow to anger."

REVIEW

The short verse, " *Let every individual be quick to listen, slow to speak and slow to anger*" is simple, yet profound, for the words are easy to understand but hard to live by.

Principle 1: Quick to listen

It is quite possible to hear but fail "to listen." Simply put, we need to listen to the message, not just hear the words. How often could we have saved ourselves a great deal of trouble if only we had truly listened to others and responded in an appropriate manner?

Principle 2: Slow to speak

All too often when we say what is on the tip of our tongues, even when it's said with the best of intentions, it comes out wrong when spoken too quickly. Thus, we should be slow to speak because when we speak too quickly, our message can be poorly received, misunderstood, or just plain hurtful.

Principle 3: Slow to anger

It's important to remember that the Bible doesn't forewarn us against becoming angry, but rather against becoming angry too quickly. In fact, it's appropriate to express righteous indignation over injustice or ill treatment of others.

CHAPTER 8

⁓

HEALING BROKENNESS

Life breaks us. And when we heal,
we're stronger in the broken parts.
                              — Ernest Hemingway

A family hadn't taken a vacation in years. They had a beautiful home, a fine dog, and a wonderful grandmother, and they just didn't feel as though they could leave unless someone was around to look after them.

One day a dear friend said, "I've noticed that you never get away. You need to." They told the friend that they didn't have anyone to look after their house, their dog, or their grandmother while they were away. The friend volunteered to take care of all three, and they accepted his generous offer.

The family had been away for several days when they felt they needed to check in with their friend. When they called, he seemed quite relieved to be talking with them.

"How are things going?" the vacationing father inquired.

"Your dog died," the friend responded.

"You can't just tell us that our dog died," the father said indignantly. "You have to be more compassionate, more sensitive than that. You need to break the news to us more gently.

"Today you should have said 'Your dog is on the roof.' And then tomorrow you should have said, 'Your dog fell off the roof.' The third day you should have said, 'Your dog is at the vet, and they're doing the best they can to save him.' And then on the fourth day you could tell me, 'Your dog died.'"

"You're right," the friend responded. "I'm so sorry. I promise that I'll do better next time because I sincerely want to be more sensitive and compassionate."

"May I speak to Grandmother?" the father asked.

There was a long pause on the other end before the friend replied gently, "No, I wish you could, but she can't come to the phone right now."

"What do you mean she can't come to the phone. Where is she?"

"She's on the roof," came the reply.

No News Is Good News

The story is a humorous reminder that we don't like to hear bad news. And yet the truth of the matter is that we can't find a solution to a problem until we recognize the problem; and we can't hear the good news until we've heard the bad news.

The bad news is that today we live in a world of brokenness. Because we haven't been good stewards of nature, for example, the environment is "broken" with pollution. I remember taking my son Chaz on a Cub Scout camping trip to a state park a few years ago. When we went to fill up our canteens from a water spigot in the park, I couldn't believe what was written on a sign underneath the faucet: "This water isn't suitable for drinking."

Amazingly, there are hundreds of sites all over the world where entire communities have been relocated because of the hazardous wastes in and around their neighborhood. To make matters worse, compared to most countries, America is pristine and pollution free. If you've read anything about the horrendous pollution throughout the former communist countries in Eastern Europe, you'll understand exactly what I mean.

Several years ago when I lived in Jacksonville, Florida, the local newspapers reported that our county, Duval, had the number one cancer rate in the nation. Some experts theorized the high cancer rate was caused by worldwide air streams that passed over Jacksonville, depositing pollution from around the world. This theory isn't far-fetched, as evidenced by the fact that Jacksonville was one of only five cities in the United States which registered radioactive fallout from the Chernobyl Nuclear Power Plant in the Soviet Union.

Broken Relationships

Pollution is caused by a broken relationship between humans and nature. If, instead, we humans would honor our relationship with nature and nurture it, everything would be fine. But when we start tampering with the relationship out of greed or neglect, it breaks the bond between us, and both humans and nature suffer the consequences.

Pollution is a serious problem as we enter the 21st century, that's for sure. But this chapter isn't just about the *problems* of broken relationships, per se. This chapter is about arriving at *solutions* to broken relationships. In a word, what we'll be looking at is the process of healing our broken relationships through *reconciliation*.

RECONCILIATION: COMING TOGETHER AGAIN

The Bible teaches that there are two great commandments of life and faith. First, "You shall love the Lord your God with all your heart and mind and soul and strength;" the second commandment reads, "You shall love your neighbor as yourself."

When I talk about healing broken relationships, I'm really talking about honoring these two commandments, for in order for us to enjoy the rewards of the abundant life, our relationship with God and with our fellow humans must be whole.

It's been my observation that the tallest, most difficult walls for us to climb are the walls of broken relationships. But climb them we must, for we need to heal the broken relationships between God and ourselves — and between our neighbors and ourselves — if we want to become whole again.

The Definition of Reconciliation

Reconciliation is defined by its two roots. The first syllable, *re*, means "again or anew." The second root, *conciliation*, comes from the word "council" and means "together." Reconciliation, therefore, means "to bring together again."

The connotation is, of course, that what once was whole has been torn apart; and, therefore, it must be brought together again because our lives must be whole in order for us to live abundantly.

What Happens When We Don't Reconcile

The best way to help you understand the perils of not reconciling is to tell you the story of how the Horns of Bebenhausen became famous throughout Europe.

On the wall of an old monastery near Bebenhausen, Germany, is a spectacular display of deer horns mounted on an old plaque. Upon closer inspection, visitors invariably notice that the display isn't one pair of huge horns; rather it's two pairs of horns locked together.

It seems that many years ago a monk from the monastery found the two sets of horns in a forest near Bebenhausen. Apparently, two bucks had been fighting, and their horns had become so entangled during their battle that they couldn't be separated. And so, ironically, the two died as mortal enemies, locked together forever.

We are destined to the same fate as the two bucks unless we engage in the process of reconciliation, whether the broken relationship is with our God, with our spouse, with a former friend, with a business competitor, or whomever.

God Works in Mysterious Ways

As we're all aware, God works in mysterious ways, most especially in His efforts to help people heal the broken relationships in their lives. Max Cleland is a case in point.

Cleland is a United Methodist layman and a United States Senator from Georgia who lost both legs in Vietnam as he tried to rescue an army buddy during combat. This tragedy was a major blow to Max, of course.

But as Cleland started on his long road to recovery, he was forced to reassess his life and his values. As a result, he developed a new perspective on what was most important in his life.

Cleland believes his life is more abundant today than it was before his injury, for he has come to appreciate the rewards of putting his relationships ahead of himself.

A huge wall was placed in Cleland's life when he lost his legs. But I believe that wall was placed there so that Max Cleland could use it as a "stepping stone" to help himself climb an even higher wall — the wall of reconciliation.

Detours on the Path to Reconciliation

Humans have an inborn need to belong, which is why the quality of our relationships with others will determine the quality of the lives we live. Unfortunately, there is a great deal of brokenness and estrangement in the world today in the form of racism, sexism, nationalism, denominationalism, and the like. This is why so many of us lack a sense of joy and fulfillment in life.

Some people try to fill the vacuum of their brokenness with money or power or recognition, believing that if they can only HAVE enough, they can BE whole again. But, alas, they remain unhappy, for the vacuum can't be filled from the outside — it can only be filled from within.

Others seek to escape from the brokenness of life through drug and alcohol abuse, but, once again, they remain unhappy because narcotics can't fill the void either. And some people, in a fit of desperation, seek the ultimate escape, suicide.

You see, none of these efforts can ever cover up the pain of brokenness. The only way to make the pain go away is to heal the brokenness. And that, my friend, is what reconciliation is all about.

There are four steps that we must take if we want to experience reconciliation in our lives. They are as follows:

Step 1) Recognizing the problem

Step 2) Restoring the relationship

Step 3) Responding to restoration

Step 4) Renewal and wholeness

Let's talk about each of these steps in a little more depth.

STEP 1: RECOGNIZING THE PROBLEM

Not long ago I saw a cartoon featuring two cute junior high girls walking home from school. One girl sees a handsome boy from the local high school walking on the other side of the street. She nudges her friend, exclaiming, "Look, there goes your boyfriend, Gregory!"

"Oh, Gregory and I aren't speaking any more," the second girl responds. "I've lost all interest in him. We haven't spoken for three days, six hours, and forty-three minutes."

How often do we act like the young girl in the cartoon, refusing to admit that we have hurt — or have been hurt by — someone else. Consequently, we avoid the problem, allowing it to smolder until it either creates total estrangement or erupts into violence. Both responses could have been easily avoided if the problem had been recognized and dealt with earlier.

The Power of Confession

Bishop Fulton J. Sheen, the Catholic priest who introduced Christianity to television in the 1950s, once visited Dr. Schuller's Garden Grove Community Church. Sheen was impressed with the drive-in facilities, where people could drive to church but remain in their cars to hear the message.

Sheen commended Schuller on this concept, and then with a twinkle in his eye told Schuller he was going to introduce the concept to the Catholic Church. Sheen humorously suggested that Catholic churches would begin with drive-in confessionals. They could install a drive-in window on the side of every Catholic church in America with a sign above it that said, "Toot and tell, or go to hell."

Sheen was joking, of course, but the confessional within the Catholic church does play an important part in the reconciliation process in that it requires parishioners to reflect upon their lives and confess their sins regularly.

Breakdown in Communication

From my experience as a counselor, I'd have to say that the number one cause of divorce among couples today is poor communication. Without a doubt, lack of communication is the tallest wall between couples, as well as the hardest to build a door through.

That's why in my premarital counseling sessions, I spend a good deal of time with couples discussing the different levels of communication so that the future husband and wife can become more aware of how breakdowns in communication can lead to a marital breakdown.

Furthermore, I tell the couples that if they'll always recognize a given problem and then work toward its resolution before going to bed, they'll set the wheels of reconciliation in motion. Failure to do so sets the wheels of estrangement in motion. The first step in reconciliation is to recognize that a problem exists, either on your behalf or on behalf of the other person.

STEP 2: RESTORING THE RELATIONSHIP

The second step to reconciliation is RESTORATION!

Restoration doesn't mean that the problem is resolved once and for all. But it does mean that one or both parties are making an effort to restore the relationship to its prior status. This can be difficult for us because it requires that we set aside our pride and seek or offer forgiveness. And, quite often, this is made even more difficult by the fact that many individuals who need reconciliation don't recognize their ill deeds, much less their need for forgiveness.

Take a Win/Win Approach

The great Methodist preacher, Wallace Hamilton, told the story of an Indian sheep farmer who had a problem with his neighbor. It seems that the neighbor owned a pack of dogs that were allowed to roam freely, and they were continually killing the Indian's sheep.

The Indian thoughtfully considered all the alternatives available to him. He could bring a lawsuit against his neighbor, but that would be costly and would alienate the neighbor. Or he could build stronger fences to keep the dogs out, but that would require a lot more time and money than he had, so he didn't want to do that either.

Then the Indian thought of an ingenious plan that would not only solve the problem, but would permanently heal their broken relationship. One afternoon the Indian walked over to his neighbor's house and gave four little lambs to his neighbor's children.

When the neighbor saw how much his children loved the lambs, he voluntarily tied up his dogs so that the lambs would be safe. The sheep farmer's problems were over.

I love how the Indian in this story solved a problem that was on the brink of exploding into violence. I'm sure the Indian's first response was to shoot the renegade dogs, but he had the good sense to know that an act of violence would just escalate their problems. Because the Indian was "slow to anger," he arrived at a solution that worked out beautifully for both parties. This story is wall-climbing and door-building at it's best!

As the Indian fully understood, the Golden Rule of life and of relationships is this: "Do unto others as you would have others do unto you." Unlike most ethical rules for life, the Golden Rule doesn't tell you what you should NOT do. It tells you what you SHOULD do. The secret of the Golden Rule is that it forces us to put ourselves in the other person's shoes, and when we do that, we're taking a major step toward restoring the relationship.

STEP 3: RESPONDING TO RESTORATION

The third step to reconciliation is RESPONSE!

It's not enough for one party to make a gesture to restore a broken relationship. Once someone offers a peace pipe, so to speak, both parties have to be willing to sit down and smoke it or the broken relationship will never truly heal.

It's like the story of the 17-year-old cat who caught her last bird. By that age, the old cat moved too slowly to be much of a threat to the birds in the neighborhood anymore. So she was as surprised as the bird when she managed to catch a sparrow while it was napping on her lawn.

The old cat immediately took her catch to the back door of the house and purred that familiar purr that said to her master, "Come see what I have caught."

The master was relieved to discover that the sparrow wasn't injured. Although the sparrow's feathers were ruffled and she was in a state of mild shock, there was actually very little damage that a 17-year-old cat with one tooth could do.

Response Is a Two-Way Street

The master placed the bird in the middle of the lawn and waited for it to take off. Almost an hour passed, and the sparrow still remained crouched in the middle of the yard. Finally, the master gently picked up the bird and flung it high into the air. The bird responded by flying away.

The point of the story is that reconciliation demands a response on the part of both parties. The master tried to make amends for the injuries the bird received from the cat, but restitution couldn't occur until the bird was willing to fly. Without the bird's willingness to accept the master's restitution in full, reconciliation would never have been possible.

In a like manner, there will be times in our own lives when reconciliation doesn't take place right away. We've all suffered emotional injuries where we chose to sit around like the bird, rather than accept the offending party's apologies. The truth is, it may take time for the wounds to heal, so sitting around can serve a very useful purpose.

And yet, there comes a time when the injured party has to act, too. Whether we're the one extending the olive branch to someone we've hurt or whether we're on the receiving end, it takes two people to make a reconciliation work.

The person seeking to heal the broken relationship must, at the very least, plant the seeds of reconciliation, recognizing that just as a seed doesn't grow into a tree overnight, neither do broken relationships heal overnight. But at some point, the person receiving the peace offering must open a door through his wall of resistance so that true healing can begin.

STEP 4: RENEWAL AND WHOLENESS

Once we have recognized the need for reconciliation and have taken steps toward restoring the previous relationship, and once the other party has responded positively to our efforts, then, and only then, can the final stage of reconciliation take place — renewal and wholeness.

Reconcile Before It's Too Late

A friendly rivalry between two great English novelists, William M. Thackeray and Charles Dickens, escalated into a bitter quarrel. Their quarrel escalated to such a point that in 1863, when they met in person in London, they agreed never to speak to one another again.

Thackeray realized immediately, however, that he couldn't bear the division between them, and as Dickens turned to leave, Thackeray ran after Dickens, seized his hand, and begged him to reconsider, for he simply couldn't bear the coldness between them. The two men shook hands, and healed the breech between them.

With one sincere act, Thackeray was able to dispel the jealousy and anger between him and a man he admired enormously, and their previous relationship was renewed.

Not long thereafter Thackeray died. Sir Thomas Martin wrote these words of that event in his memoirs: "The next time I saw Dickens he was standing at the grave of his rival. He must have rejoiced, I thought, that he had shaken hands so warmly a few days before."

This episode confirms the power of the reconciliation process. It must have been hard for a proud man like Thackeray to run after his rival and announce publicly that he couldn't stand the coldness between them. It must have been equally difficult for Dickens to put his enmity behind him at a moment's notice. But both men did what was necessary to heal their broken relationship, and in the end, both men were better off for it.

A Classic Story of Reconciliation

One of the great classics of Western literature, *A Christmas Carol* by Charles Dickens, is the best example of the process of reconciliation that I can think of. I'm convinced that the reason Dickens' story is told and retold, year after year, is because it captures the very heart of reconciliation. In fact, the story outlines perfectly the three stages necessary for reconciliation:

First, Scrooge *recognizes* the brokenness that exists in the world between him and each of his neighbors when he is visited by the three ghosts of Christmas past, present, and future.

Secondly, he *restores* the broken relationships with genuine gestures of generosity and giving.

Thirdly, his "friends" and employees *respond* to his efforts when they openly accept his changed disposition, his willingness to give, and his desire to be with them.

And finally, all of the characters experience *renewal and wholeness* as a result of Scrooge's change of heart, and life takes on a new sense of hope, peace, joy, and fulfillment for everyone as Tiny Tim closes the story with his refrain, "God bless us everyone."

REVIEW

Reconciliation is defined by its two roots. The first syllable, *re*, means "again or anew." The second root, *conciliation*, is derived from the word "council" and means "together." Reconciliation, therefore, means "to bring together again." The meaning is, of course, that what once was whole is torn apart and must be made whole again.

Reconciliation is necessary in human relationships whenever individuals have become entangled with one another in bitterness and hatred or estranged from one another because of some perceived ill will or ill deed. In such cases as these, reconciliation is essential to save the relationship that once existed.

Principle 1: Recognize the problem

We live in a world that is torn apart by the breakdown of our relationships with others, and, therefore, reconciliation is necessary to restore the intended harmony that should exist in our relationships.

The first step in climbing the wall of reconciliation is to recognize that a problem exists, either on your behalf or on behalf of another.

Principle 2: Restore the relationship

The second step in reconciliation is restoration. Restoration doesn't mean that the problem is resolved, but it does mean that one or more people are making an effort to restore the relationship to its previous status.

This principle can be difficult for us because it requires that we set aside our pride and seek forgiveness or offer forgiveness. And, quite often, this is made even more difficult by the fact that the individual who we're seeking to reconcile with may not recognize either his ill deed or his need for forgiveness.

Principle 3: Respond to restoration

The third step in reconciliation is a response. There will be times in our own lives in which a wounded person won't respond to us right away. In fact, it may take time for the wounds to heal. And yet, people seeking to heal the broken relationship in life must, at the very least, plant the seeds of reconciliation, recognizing that just as a seed doesn't become a tree overnight, neither do relationships become whole all at once.

Principle 4: Experience renewal and wholeness

Once we've recognized the need for reconciliation and have taken steps toward restoring a relationship, and once the other party has affirmed our efforts by responding to us, then renewal takes place, which is the final stage of reconciliation. When renewal occurs, the richness and wholeness of life return through the relationships that we share.

PART 3

~

On the Other Side of the Wall

Reflect on your present blessings, of which every man has plenty; not on your past misfortunes, of which all men have some.
— Charles Dickens

CHAPTER 9

~

EXCELLING IN LIFE THROUGH LOVE

*To laugh often and much; to win the respect of intel-
ligent people and the affection of children; to earn
the appreciation of honest critics and endure the betrayal of false friends; to appreciate beauty; to find
the best in others; to leave the world a bit better,
whether by a healthy child, a garden patch or a re-
deemed social condition; to know even one life has
breathed easier because you have lived: This is to
have succeeded.*

— Ralph Waldo Emerson

Charles M. Schwab was 72 years old when he was
sued for a large sum of money. Because he was one of the wealthiest
men of his day, it made sense to settle out of court.

He decided to fight the suit in court, however, and he won. On the
day that he testified on his own behalf, Schwab asked the judge if he
could make a statement before leaving the stand. The judge agreed.

Schwab addressed the courtroom, saying, "I'm an old man, and I
want to say that 90 percent of my troubles have been due to my being
good to other people. If you younger folk want to avoid trouble, be

hard-boiled and say 'no' to everybody. You will then walk through life unmolested.

"But," and here the old-time smile lit up his face, "you'll have to do without friends, and you won't have much fun."

More to Life Than Making Money

Schwab understood that accomplishments, achievements, and acquisitions are important, but he understood they aren't ends in themselves. Rewards and material things are important only if they're used as a means to nourishing relationships with others.

Aristotle Onassis was one individual who learned the limitations of worldly riches. At the height of his powers, Onassis was one of the richest, most powerful men in the world. He had everything money could buy, including the world's most glamorous women.

"All that really counts these days is money," he once boasted. "It's the people with money who are the royalty today."

He eventually came to understand the emptiness of that boast. Onassis learned the hard way that there are some things money can't buy, for his only son, Alexander, was killed in a plane crash.

A close associate said the sudden tragedy changed Onassis overnight: "He suddenly became an old man," the associate reported. "In business negotiations he was uncharacteristically absent-minded, irrational, and petulant."

Ironically, the one thing that Onassis valued the most — his son's life — was also the one thing he couldn't buy back.

Love Cures People

We only truly excel in life when we love, because when it's all said and done, love is the reason we climb the walls and build the doors in our lives. Love is the greatest motivator and the greatest payoff in the world.

Think about it. If people really and truly could express — and accept — love unconditionally, do you think our prisons would be overflowing? Do you think one out of two marriages would end in divorce? Do you think child abuse would be epidemic? Do you think people would consume tons and tons of antidepressants every single year? Of course not!

Dr. Karl Menninger, one of the pioneers of modern psychiatry and the founder of the world-famous Menninger Clinic, had this to say about our inborn need for love:

"Love cures people — both the ones who give it and the ones who receive it." Menninger's life long experience as a psychiatrist convinced him that true excellence in life can only be achieved through love, for he observed firsthand that people can't cure their brokenness without love.

Love Is a Warm Lap

Children have a wonderful way of bringing home reality. I recently heard of a high-powered businessman who grew tired of reading his daughter bedtime stories. Being a resourceful businessman, however, the father thought he came up with a perfect solution.

He bought his daughter a cassette player and recorded all of her favorite stories on tape, figuring this solution would give him more time to work at home while his daughter could still hear her stories.

But, much to his amazement, his daughter wasn't happy at all. When she asked him to read the stories again, he inquired, "Have you lost the tape player I bought you?"

"No," she responded quietly.

"Well, then, what's the matter?" he questioned.

"The tape player doesn't have a lap," she responded innocently.

This story is a poignant reminder that "things" can never take the place of human relationships. The little girl loved to be touched by the stories. But even more, she loved the touch of the storyteller, her father.

The Greatest of These Is Love

We are reminded throughout the Bible that love is the most important ingredient for living an abundant life: As the Bible says,

"Faith, hope and love, abide these three, but the greatest of these is love."

But have you ever stopped to ask yourself why, among those qualities that God considers essential to the abundant life — faith, hope, and love — love is the greatest?

In the following pages we'll look at the five fundamental principles that make love the key to excellence.

LOVE IS COMPASSIONATE

Dwight W. Morrow, the father of Anne Lindbergh, was hosting a small dinner party when the conversation turned to the race for president of the United States. Morrow voiced his support for his friend Calvin Coolidge, but several dinner companions remained unimpressed.

They complained that Coolidge lacked flair, was too unassuming, and had no political personality.

"Why should we support a candidate that no one likes?" asked one guest.

"I liked him," chimed in Morrow's six-year-old daughter, Anne. Then she lifted up her bandaged finger and continued, "He was the only one who asked me about my sore finger."

Her father smiled at his daughter, turned to his guests and said, "There's your answer."

The point of the story is that people always remember acts of compassion. That's what the expression, "What comes around, goes around" is all about. More often than not, if you treat people with respect and courtesy, you get the same in return.

LOVE GIVES COMFORT

Charles Allen, in his book *Home Fires*, recounts the story of a man who tells his wife one morning that today is the day he's going to ask his boss for a raise. The husband nervously avoids his boss all day, but finally, near closing time, he manages to muster up enough courage to ask his boss for a raise.

To the husband's surprise, the boss agrees not only to give the husband a bigger raise than he asks for, but praises him highly as well! When the husband arrives home that night he's surprised again, for his wife has prepared a romantic candlelight dinner just for the occasion.

"Honey," he exclaims to his wife, "I got the raise, but I see by the table that you already knew. Great, I'm ready to celebrate!" They embrace, and as he sits down at the table, he notices a note that reads: "Congratulations, darling! I knew you'd get the raise. This dinner will tell you how much I love you."

The dinner is delicious. As his wife is clearing the table for dessert, the husband notices a note stuck to the bottom of her plate fall to the floor. He picks up the note and reads:

"Don't worry about not getting the raise, my dear, even though you deserved it. This dinner will tell you how much I love you."

At that moment he realizes that his wife loved him and supported him whether he got the raise or not. She rejoiced in the good news, but she was ready to comfort her husband if the news was bad. Because she understood that love gives comfort, her husband appreciated her more than ever before.

LOVE SHARES CONCERNS

Love is the greatest of all attributes because it shares concerns. What a difference it makes when people genuinely care about one another and act on that concern.

There's an ancient Hebrew legend that reveals the fullness of what I mean when I say love shares concerns. Many years ago two brothers lived side by side on adjoining lands.

One brother had a large family and the other lived alone. The married brother lay awake one night and thought to himself, "My brother the bachelor does not have the companionship of a wife nor children to cheer his heart. While he sleeps, I will carry some of my sheaves of wheat and place them in his field."

The brother who was a bachelor was also laying awake in thought that night: "My brother has a large family and his needs are greater than mine. As he sleeps, I will carry some of my sheaves and place them in his field."

Thus, both brothers went out, gathered sheaves of their own to place in the other's field, and met each other at the dividing line of their property. When the brothers realized what they had done, they laughed and embraced. And according to the legend, years later the Jerusalem Temple was built on the dividing line of the brothers' properties, and the altar stood where they embraced.

We learn from this story what true abundance is all about, for each brother was rich in love and concern for his sibling, and their selfless concern meant more to them than all the wheat in the world.

LOVE CONQUERS ALL

Love is the greatest of all attributes because love conquers all. Love never fails us in times of sorrow, and it is so powerful that it bridges the differences between us. The following two true stories document how love conquers all.

Years ago in Victorian England, William Dixon lived alone in the small village of Brackenthwaite, having lost both his wife and his son to death.

One day he noticed a neighbor's house on fire. Although the aged owner was rescued, her orphaned grandson was trapped in the blaze. Dixon climbed up an iron pipe on the side of the house and lowered the boy to safety.

The iron pipe was red hot, however, and as a result, both of Dixon's hands were badly burned. Several years after the rescue, the grandmother passed away, and the townspeople debated over who should take care of her grandchild.

The town council called a meeting to settle the matter, and two men offered to take care of the boy. The first man had lost his son, and wanted to adopt the orphan. He gave an eloquent speech as to why the young boy should live with him. Everyone on the council was very moved, and it looked like the man had won the day.

The other man who sought to take care of the boy was Dixon, the man who had saved him from the fire. When it was Dixon's turn to speak, he approached the town council but said nothing. His only testimony was to lift up his scarred hands. The town council voted unanimously that Dixon should adopt the child.

In the end, the scars of love conquered whatever skepticism the town council may have had about Dixon's ability to care for the child.

Loves Bridges Our Differences

The second story concerns a dedicated young preacher in the 1800s who walked 20 miles to deliver a sermon to a small congregation in rural Missouri.

By the time the preacher arrived, he was exhausted. To complicate matters, this was his first sermon, and he was so nervous that he stammered and failed to remember even the most familiar verses.

The congregation was disappointed by his sermon, and unaware of his long journey, not a single church member offered the preacher food or shelter. As he prepared to make the long walk back home, the black church janitor asked the young preacher to share a humble meal in his shanty nearby. The preacher gratefully accepted.

Years passed and the young preacher became the renowned Bishop

Marvin. Again he returned to that little country church. It was a big event in that little church's life to have a man of Bishop Marvin's caliber preach to them. Everyone in the town agreed it was the best sermon they had ever heard in their lives. After the service, the townspeople all filed outside to shake the Bishop's hand and to offer their most lavish hospitality.

The Bishop thanked them politely but declined each invitation. Then he startled the conservative cititzens of that small, segregated city by gesturing to the black janitor to join him for dinner with these words: "When I was here years ago, I was none too good for you. And I am none too good for you today."

The point of the story is that with love, all things are possible. Love reaches across social and racial divides and binds us together, no matter what our differences. Love conquers the difficult, the skeptical, and the differences that separate us. In a word, love conquers all.

Love is the greatest of all attributes because it feels compassion, it gives comfort, it shares concern and it always conquers. Love nourishes human relationships and enables them to grow and mature. But, in order for us to truly experience love and to share it, we must first learn the ways of love.

LOVE MUST BE EFFECTIVELY COMMUNICATED

Climbing the walls in our lives is risky business. We suffer lots of scratches, bruises, and broken bones when we fall off the scaffolding. The great thing about love is it helps cushion the fall. There's nothing quite like the feeling of having someone in our corner when we fall down and scrape our knees.

But it seems like the line from the old song, "You always hurt the one you love, the one you didn't want to hurt at all," is sad, but true. It's been my experience that it's not the love that does the hurting so much as it is our failure to understand how to express that love.

Ironically, one of the biggest walls that you'll have to climb in your life is the wall of communication that exists between you and your spouse, for unless love is appropriately expressed, it will stack up like a wall of bricks until it becomes insurmountable.

Three Different Ways of Saying "I Love You"

Just as there are different types of love, there are different ways of expressing love, and it's important for us to be aware of this. Without a doubt, the biggest challenge facing married couples today is a lack of communication.

John Gray's best-selling book *Men Are From Mars, Women Are From Venus*, talked about how the differences between men and women make it seem like we are speaking different languages when we try to communicate. To complicate matters, psychologists tell us that people have different communication styles. The three basic personality styles are affective, verbal, and active.

Depending on the communication style of the listener, the message "I love you" would best be communicated in three different ways. The best way to communicate with a person who is verbal, for example, is simply to say, "I love you."

The best way to communicate "I love you" to an affective person, on the other hand, is to arrange a romantic evening or a walk along the river holding hands.

To best communicate your love for an active person, you need not be as concerned with what you say or with setting the mood with romance. For active people, actions speak louder than words. Active people receive the message of love when you go by and pick up their clothes from the laundry without their having to ask you to, for example.

Interestingly enough, none of us are purely active or affective or verbal. We each possess all three styles, although one of the three is usually much more dominant than the others. However, it's important that you recognize the dominance so that you can communicate your love to the other on their level.

For example, I'm an active person, and if my wife gave me a flower arrangement for Valentine's Day, I'd think it was a waste of money. I would rather have a tool from Sears or a new gadget for my computer.

On the other hand, my wife would be horrified if I gave her a microwave for the kitchen. I know from experience, because I tried it on our first anniversary. My wife is affective, and she would much rather receive flowers than a practical gift. Someone who was verbal, however, would probably be happier if you expressed your love in a letter or poem.

If one person is affective and another is active, then communication can become a huge, unclimbable wall unless each understands how best to communicate in the spouse's style.

When Verbal and Affective Marry

I performed the marriage ceremony for a young Navy couple some time ago, and shortly after the wedding, the young man was stationed in Italy for six months. It was very important that they communicate their love to one another on the appropriate level or else they could begin to question what they were hearing one another say.

When he returned from Italy, they were having troubles and didn't understand why. It seems the "verbal" wife had been writing daily love letters to her "active" husband, who was buying practical gifts on his shore leave for his affective wife. As a result, both were communicating their love but neither was hearing what the other was saying.

The wife was verbal-affective, and what she wanted was a love letter she could share with her girlfriends, revealing her husband's love for her. The husband was active, and what he needed was a box of cookies that he could share with his buddies and to show what his wife had done for him.

Their love was genuine, and both the husband and the wife tried their best to communicate in the "language" of their spouse. The next time they were apart, she sent cookies, and he sent love letters. All is fine now.

In an era in which relationships are becoming more and more complex, it's crucial that we learn to effectively communicate our feelings to one another.

REVIEW

Love is the greatest of all attributes because it feels compassion, it gives comfort, it shares concerns, and it always conquers. Love nourishes human relationships and enables them to grow and mature.

We can excel in life through love by understanding and honoring five key principles:

Principle 1: Love is compassionate

People always remember acts of compassion. Random acts of kindness can help revitalize people's souls and remind them that, at some time or the other, we all need someone to understand our hurt.

Principle 2: Love gives comfort

Love understands that we're to rejoice in the good news, but we must be ready to comfort our loved ones when the news is bad.

Principle 3: Love shares concerns

Love is the greatest of all attributes because it shares concerns. What a difference it makes when people genuinely care about one another and act on that concern.

Principle 4: Love conquers all

Love reaches across social and racial divides and binds us together, no matter what our differences. Love conquers the difficult, the skeptical, and the differences that separate us. In a word, love conquers all.

Principle 5: Love must be effectively communicated

Ironically, one of the biggest walls that you'll have to climb in your life is the wall of communication that exists between you and your spouse, for unless love is appropriately expressed, it will stack up like a wall of bricks until it becomes insurmountable.

CHAPTER 10

⌒

CELEBRATING LIFE

*We tend to forget that happiness doesn't come as a
result of getting something we don't have, but rather
of recognizing and appreciating what we do have.*
— Frederick Keonig

In early New England, it was the custom to place five
kernels of corn at every plate during the Thanksgiving meal as a reminder of that first dreadful winter the Pilgrims spent in America.

During that first winter, all but seven of the passengers and crew
of the *Mayflower* became ill. Food was so scarce that it was rationed,
and at one point the daily ration was only five kernels of corn. By the
end of that winter, nearly half of the group had died.

And yet, when the *Mayflower* returned home, only the crew chose to return to England. All the passengers stayed, proving that the Pilgrims were willing to risk their lives for freedom.

The tradition of placing five kernels of corn at every plate was a way for the Pilgrims to remind everyone of the huge sacrifice their forefathers made so that future generations could enjoy freedom.

THE CONDITIONS FOR A THANKFUL HEART

Our circumstances and conditions are far removed from those of the Pilgrims who celebrated the first Thanksgiving Day in 1621. They had, in the previous year, lost a ship, endured severe health problems, been attacked by Indians, and lost nearly half of the original 102 passengers who journeyed to the New World on the *Mayflower*. And yet, in the midst of their hardship, they found time to give thanks to God for his blessings.

Be Thankful for What You've Got

How different was their story from the story Winston Churchill liked to tell about a man who risked his life to save a drowning child. When the man returned the child home, the mother snapped, "Where's Johnny's cap?"

The mother had so much to be thankful for, and yet, she chose to focus on the small item that was lost, instead of the life that was saved. On the other hand, the Pilgrims appeared to have so little to be thankful for, and yet they celebrated. How can this be? The answer is really quite simple, for, you see, a spirit of thanksgiving arises out of an attitude of gratitude and not out of one's condition in life.

Have you noticed that some people concentrate so hard on climbing walls and building doors in their lives that they don't take the time to celebrate when they finally arrive on the other side of the wall? What a shame!

If we don't stop to celebrate the small victories in our lives by giving thanks for our daily blessings, then we're destined to spend most of our time being unhappy, for the big blessings are few and far between.

A genuine spirit of thanksgiving always recognizes the blessings of life, no matter how small. It doesn't get caught up in saying, "I can't give thanks *because of*" ... or "I would be able to give thanks *if only.*" A genuine spirit of thanksgiving recognizes our numerous blessings and gives thanks for them.

On his 84th birthday, the famed pianist, Arthur Rubinstein, said, "As long as we have what we have inside, the capacity to love, to work, to hear music, to see a flower, to look at the world as it is, nothing can stop us from being happy ... but one thing you must take seriously. You must get rid of the 'ifs' of life. Many people tell you, 'I would be happy IF I had a certain job, or IF I were better looking, or IF a certain person would marry me.' There isn't any such thing. You must live your life unconditionally, without the ifs."

A spirit of thanksgiving arises from an attitude of gratitude within the heart. It doesn't arise out of our condition in life, for we can always look at where we are and find reasons to be thankful, as well as reasons not to be. Howard Hughes had wealth, but he wasn't happy. Mother Teresa lived in the worst slums in the world, and yet she was happy, proving that an attitude of gratitude results from what's happening IN us, rather than what's happening TO us.

THE BLESSINGS OF A THANKFUL HEART

The thankful heart colors our world by making us aware of the many blessings we have received. When we don't give thanks, we end up taking things for granted, and, as a result, we don't experience the richness of our blessings.

It's like the story of the tourist who took an extended tour of Mexico. He was amazed to discover that in certain parts of the country, natural hot and cold springs existed side by side.

In these regions, it's not necessary for the local villagers to boil water to wash clothes. Instead, the locals take their dirty laundry to the natural springs, where they can wash it in the hot springs and rinse it in the cold.

Upon witnessing this phenomenon, the tourist said to the guide, "I guess the people here think Mother Nature is pretty special to supply both hot and cold water, side by side, for their personal use?"

"Oh, no, señor," the tour guide responded. "There is much grumbling because she supplies no soap."

This story illustrates that we humans were born with a bottomless pit when it comes to our expectations. It seems like no matter how much we get, we always want more. That's why we must consciously remind ourselves to take time for thanksgiving. We're all born selfish by nature, and unless we program ourselves to take time to celebrate life, we run the risk of always being unhappy.

Even the Food Tastes Better

Fulton Oursler tells the story about Anna, the family housekeeper and nurse who cared for him as a child. She taught him one of the greatest lessons of all, and that was the importance of giving thanks.

One day as they were seated for dinner, the housekeeper folded her hands, and said, "Much obliged, Lord, for the victuals."

"What are 'vittles'?" the young Fulton asked.

"The 'vittles' are what I've got to eat and drink," she replied

"But you'd have 'vittles' whether you thanked the Lord or not," said Fulton.

"Sure you would, but they taste better after you say thanks," she smiled.

After dinner she gave thanks again and then said to Fulton, "Funny thing about giving thanks. You don't know how many things you have to be thankful for until you go looking for them, so I try to give thanks for everything so I can realize just how much I have to be thankful for."

Years passed and Fulton decided to visit Anna, who was dying. When he walked into the hospital room, he knew she was suffering, for her hands were clasped in pain. Fulton remembered her incurable optimism during his youth, and he wondered to himself what she could have to be thankful for now as she lay dying.

At that moment she opened her eyes, lifted her voice, and said, "Much obliged Lord, for all these friends."

The story reminds us that in the end, it's not what happens to us that matters as much as how we choose to respond. When we get to the other side of our walls, we can choose to give thanks, or we can be bitter about having to climb the wall in the first place. But the fact remains, "Everything tastes better after you say thanks."

How does life taste to you?

THE PERILS OF AN UNTHANKFUL HEART

A. J. Cronin tells of a doctor in south Wales who prescribed, in certain cases, his "thank you cure."

When a patient came in filled with discouragement or pessimism, yet had no signs of serious ailment, the doctor would give him this advice: "For six weeks say 'thank you' to everyone who does anything for you and emphasize your gratitude with a smile."

If the patient responded, "No one does anything for me," the doctor would respond, "Seek and you will find." At the end of the six weeks, almost all of his pessimistic patients would return with a new outlook on life, suddenly convinced that people had become more loving and giving.

The Perils of an Unthankful Heart

The doctor in this story understood that people's attitudes were self-fulfilling prophesies. If they had a good attitude, they saw good in people. If they had a bad attitude, they saw bad.

Shakespeare was well aware of this when he wrote, "Blow, blow thou winter wind, thou art not so unkind as man's ingratitude." A person with an unthankful heart, therefore, places a curse on his own existence. The only antidote I know of to remedy an unthankful heart is for us to set aside time to express our thankfulness for all our blessings, both large and small.

THE THANKFUL HEART MUST FIND EXPRESSION

It's important to be thankful for our blessings, that's for sure. But it's equally important to express our thanks to others. We get so busy with our lives that we forget to thank the people who bring joy to our lives.

It's like the story of the little boy who attended a birthday party for his friend, Billy. The boy's mother gave her son strict instructions to thank Billy's mother for inviting him to the party. When the mother picked up her son, she asked, "Did you thank Billy's mother for the party?"

"I was going to," her son responded. "But the boy in front of me thanked her first and she said, 'Don't mention it' — and so I didn't."

All too often we are like the little boy — a big "thank you" is in order, but we fail to express it. As a result, our failure to express thanks is hurtful to the other party, a hurt that could be remedied with two words: THANK YOU!

Go out of Your Way to Say Thanks

The Theresa Boyle was the name of a Scottish trawler. One cold day in February, while the trawler was navigating the North Sea, it was attacked by a Nazi fighter plane, and it sank.

The crew of 10 managed to escape in a small lifeboat. It was extremely cold, and the crew had very little food, so after 40 hours in the open sea, the crew was too exhausted to row any further.

Ten hours later they heard the sounds of an allied airplane. The pilot spotted the lifeboat, and buzzed the crew to let them know he saw them. The pilot circled the area until he spotted two allied minesweepers and signaled for them to follow him to the open boat. The pilot remained in the area, circling the open boat until the entire crew of the sunken trawler was taken aboard. And then off he flew.

Looking back, the pilot saw a lamp signaling him to return to the minesweepers. He returned to the rescue ship and signaled down, "Is something the matter?"

"No!" the ship signaled back. "These chaps we just picked up wanted to say thank you." Tipping his wings, the pilot flew away on his patrol.

The beauty of this story is that the sailors had the presence of mind to say "thank you," even though they were starving and nearly frozen to death. The survivors knew they had been blessed, and they recognized the need to express their gratitude, dire circumstances or not.

Expressing our appreciation for the blessings we have received not only enables us to count our blessings, but it also blesses others. When we thank others for their actions, it lets them know that we value THEM, as well as THEIR ACT OR GIFT. And everyone has a need to feel appreciated.

THE THANKFUL HEART COLORS OUR WORLD

Art Linkletter once asked a little girl, "What is salt?"

"Salt is what spoils a potato when we don't put it on," the little girl responded. Isn't that a great definition of salt? *"Salt is what spoils a potato when we don't put it on."*

Well, you would say the same for gratitude.

Gratitude is what spoils life when we don't express it.

The reason for this is that the way in which we experience life has a great deal to do with the way we perceive it. In other words, if we look for excuses to be thankful, sure enough, we'll find them. If we don't, we won't. It's that simple.

You See What You're Trained to See

The story I'm about to tell you will explain what I mean.

A young farmer visited New York for the first time. He was amazed by the height of the skyscrapers and by all the people. As he was walking down a crowded avenue, he thought he heard the familiar sound of a cricket. He stopped and listened carefully. "Yep, that was a cricket."

The sound appeared to be coming from a bush in front of a large department store, so he made his way over to the large bush and began looking around. A department store employee came out and inquired, "May I help you?"

"No, thank you," replied the young man. "Just thought I heard a cricket over here."

"Oh, no," said the employee indignantly. "Not in New York City." The young farmer followed the chirping sound until he found the cricket, picked it up, and said, "Oh, yes I did, and here it is."

The young farmer was fascinated that he was the only one who heard the cricket, even though thousands of people walked by this bush every hour, so he decided to conduct a little experiment.

He reached into his pocket, pulled out a quarter, and flipped it into the air. The moment the coin hit the sidewalk, 24 people stopped in mid-walk to look for the fallen coin!

Psychologists have a word for the phenomenon that the young farmer witnessed. It's called *attending*, and it means that we can train ourselves to become aware of certain sights and sounds. People who sell shoes for a living, for example, will invariably notice the style and color of the shoes you're wearing because they are attending to shoes, but they might not have a clue as to the color of your eyes.

Big Thanks for Small Blessings

In a similar manner, we can train ourselves to become more thankful for the small blessings in our lives, and as we begin to attend to those blessings, we will see more and more things to be grateful for.

Rupert Brooke once took an inventory of the things he was grateful for. Each one brought back a fond memory, a happy thought, or a picture of joy. Here's his list of the little things he was thankful for:

white plates and cups;
wet roofs beneath lamplight;
the strong crust of friendly bread;
rainbows;
radiant raindrops in flower cups;
the cool kindliness of sheets;
the blessing of hot water;
sleep;
footprints in the dew;
oak trees;
shining horse chestnuts;
the blue smoke of wood.

Isn't that a wonderful list of things to be thankful for? We've all noticed these wondrous things — and hundreds more. But how often do we take the time to color our world by giving thanks for the beauty that surrounds us?

Think for a moment how different the world looks to people who lack an attitude of gratitude. For them, the world is colorless.

every sunset is bleached of color;
every meal is rendered bland and tasteless;
every dream is cankered;
every relationship is soured.

Look again at the two lists. Now, which one would you like to experience on a daily basis? My friend, if you will celebrate life by embracing an attitude of gratitude, you will find the rewards you are looking for on the other side of the walls in your life.

That's what I mean when I say gratitude is absolutely essential to experiencing abundant living. To paraphrase the little girl who Art Linkletter interviewed, "Gratitude is the spice that spoils life when we don't use it."

REVIEW

We spend so much of our time and energy climbing walls and building doors that we forget to celebrate when we get to the other side! In order to live an abundant life, we need to remember to be grateful for the little triumphs and the small miracles that we witness every day. There are four conditions for a thankful heart.

The blessings of a thankful heart

Only when we take time to give thanks are we truly aware of how much we have to be thankful for. We're all born selfish by nature, and unless we program ourselves to take time to celebrate life, we run the risk of always being unhappy.

The perils of an unthankful heart

If we fail to count our blessings, our lives can become filled with discouragement, pessimism, and woe. And yet, the cure for the unthankful heart is to reprogram ourselves to concentrate on noticing the flowers on a rose bush, not just the thorns.

The thankful heart must find expression

Expressing our appreciation for the blessings we've received not only enables us to count our blessings, but it also blesses others. When we thank others for what they've done, it lets them know that we value them as people, and everyone has a need to feel a sense of value and self-worth in the eyes of others.

The thankful heart colors our world

The way in which we perceive *life* has a great deal to do with the way we *experience it*. We see what we're looking for, so it stands to reason that if we start looking for the small miracles in life, we'll start seeing more and more of them — and life will become more beautiful in the process.

CHAPTER 11

∿

FACING LIFE WITH CONFIDENCE

*Man often becomes what he believes himself to be. If
I keep on saying to myself that I cannot do a certain
thing, it is possible that I may end by really becoming incapable of doing it. On the contrary, if I shall
have the belief that I can do it, I shall surely acquire
the capacity to do it, even if I may not have it at the
beginning.*

— Mahatma Gandhi

A beautiful young woman named Sherri Lansing
was walking across the street when she was struck by an automobile.
She was tossed 20 feet into the air like a sack of potatoes.

When she landed, her skull was cracked wide open. The doctors
didn't believe she would live, but she fought back, and after spending more than a year in a cast, she was well enough to go back to
work.

This woman, who was supposed to die, went on to become the
first woman to head up a major Hollywood movie studio, Para-

mount Studios. When she resigned after only three years, the Hollywood grapevine said that she was washed up.

Sherri Lansing was a survivor, though, and she went on to produce a hit film that gained her broad recognition. Today she's recognized once again as one of the top producers in the movie business. When this very talented and courageous woman was asked why she didn't give up, she simply responded, "Everybody fails. Everybody takes his knocks, but the successful keep coming back. They stay in the game." Her winning spirit and tremendous confidence enabled her to confound her critics time and again.

David and Goliath

King David, who as a youth lead the Israelites to victory over the Philistines by slaying the mighty giant, Goliath, wrote, "Though an army besiege me, my heart will not fear; though war break out against me, even then will I be confident."

David was living proof that confidence, not talent or luck, wins the battles and the wars. David's self-confidence enabled him to triumph even though the odds were stacked against him.

It was David's confidence that enabled him to battle one-on-one with a bear, to battle one-on-one with a lion, and then to challenge the mighty Goliath. And because of his confidence, when he faced off with the mighty Goliath, he didn't think to himself, "Goliath is so large I'll never have a chance." More likely he thought, "With a target that big, I can't miss!"

The lesson we learn from Sherri Lansing and King David is clear: We must have confidence in ourselves if we're serious about negotiating the walls in our lives and enjoying the abundant life on the other side.

CONFIDENCE: THE GIANT SLAYER

What is confidence? Simply put, confidence is the belief in your own ability to get the job done. Confidence is a prerequisite to living the abundant life because it enables us to see walls as temporary obstacles, instead of permanent barriers. When we have confidence, we don't say to ourselves, "IF" I can climb that wall, we say "WHEN" I climb that wall.

Pressure Comes from the Inside

Tommy Lasorda observes that confidence enables us to withstand the pressures in life. He goes on to say that pressure in life doesn't come from the outside, but from the inside. The inside pressure that one experiences is the fear of failure. Lasorda uses baseball to explain what he means:

"Let's say it's the seventh game of the World Series, and we're winning 3 to 2 in the bottom of the ninth. They have the bases loaded, two outs. Their best hitter is up.

"If we coaches have all done our jobs right, every player on the field is saying to himself, 'I want the ball hit to me! I'm going to react just as I've practiced a thousand times. Please hit the ball to me!'

"If, instead, a player says to himself, 'Geez, if it's hit to me and I miss it, we'll lose the game and the Series,' what's he really doing? He's *creating pressure*, because he's thinking about failing. You see, only when the player thinks positively can he deal with his fear of failing."

Henry Ford summed up the essence of confidence with his oft-quoted line, "If you think you can — or if you think you can't — you're right." As I see it, there are three kinds of confidence: basic confidence, genuine confidence, and ultimate confidence. Let's take a few moments to discuss each of these types of confidence in a little more depth.

BASIC CONFIDENCE

Basic confidence is the attitude that we develop as a consequence of our environment and our heredity. As we pass through life and have positive experiences, our basic confidence grows. On the other hand, when negative experiences come our way, our basic confidence wanes.

I'd like to tell you about two embarrassing incidents that occurred to two famous people in their youth. Although the incidents are similar, one had a very negative impact on a young man's life, while the other had a very positive impact. These incidents are a good example of how our basic confidence and self esteem are shaped by our childhood experiences.

Turning His Back on the Church

The first incident happened nearly 100 years ago in Croatia to a young boy named Josip Broz. Josip was an altar boy in a small country church, and one of his jobs was to serve the priest at high mass. One Sunday the boy accidentally dropped a glass cruet of wine during the middle of the church service. It smashed into pieces, spraying wine in all directions.

The village priest struck the altar boy on the cheek, and, in a gruff voice said, "Leave the altar and don't ever come back." The public embarrassment and humiliation had a dramatic impact on the boy, and he took the priest's angry words to heart. As a result of that humiliating experience, he never participated in a religious service again for as long as he lived.

Josip later adopted the name Tito, and he eventually rose through the communist ranks until he became dictator of Yugoslavia. Tito's boyhood experience eroded his basic confidence in the church, but his inborn intelligence and leadership skills enabled him to focus his confidence into a successful military career. How different his life might have become if his childhood experience in the church had been warm and loving, instead of humiliating.

Same Story, Different Priest

The second story involves a young altar boy named Peter in Peoria, Illinois, at the turn of the century. Like the young Tito, Peter dropped a cruet of wine onto a marble floor in the middle of mass. But this priest reacted very differently from the priest in Yugoslavia.

With a twinkle in his eye, Bishop John Spalding bent down next to the ashen-faced altar boy and whispered, "Someday you will be just as I am." That young man grew up to become Archbishop Fulton J. Sheen, the first person to minister on TV with his weekly live broadcast, *Life Is Worth Living*.

As you can plainly see, Bishop Sheen's positive experience increased his basic confidence in the church and paved the way for his entry into the priesthood. Tito's negative experience, on the other hand, forever eroded his basic confidence in organized religion.

These two stories illustrate how easily environmental influences can cause us to gain or lose our basic confidence in someone or something. Confidence that is based on environment or heredity alone comes and goes quickly. And that brings us to our next question. Is there a deeper form of confidence?

GENUINE CONFIDENCE

Genuine confidence runs deeper than the basic confidence we are born with or learn from our environment. Genuine confidence comes about when we choose to take charge of our own lives.

Imagine hereditary influences as the vehicle that carries us through life, and environmental influences as the road and weather conditions we must drive through. Although you may be limited somewhat by the vehicle and conditions, you're still the driver, isn't that correct? As the driver you choose the direction you take and the speed you want to go, and that puts you in charge.

When you have genuine confidence, then, you — and only you — take charge of your life, rather than allowing your environmental and genetic conditions to determine your final destination, as evidenced by the next story.

Dummy Becomes a Doctor

A little boy named Ben lived in Detroit with his brother and his mother. His mother had married at the age of 13 but divorced shortly after Ben was born. The kids at school made fun of Ben, and his nickname in fifth grade was "The Dummy."

Ben's mother became concerned about the treatment her two sons were receiving at school, so she required them to write her two book reports each week. As a result, Ben and his brother became familiar with the Detroit Public Library. One day in science class, the teacher raised up a shiny, black rock and asked if anyone could identify it. Only one person raised his hand. It was Ben.

His classmates giggled and chuckled because they knew "The Dummy" was about to make a fool of himself. To everyone's amazement, Ben not only correctly identified the rock, he explained how it was formed. The class was flabbergasted and Ben realized for the first time that he wasn't "The Dummy."

Ben says he'll never forget that day because he liked the way he felt when he gave the correct answer. So he decided that he'd begin reading books on every subject. By the sixth grade he had risen to the top of his class. He did well in high school and went on to graduate from both Yale University and the University of Michigan Medical School.

Ben's full name is Dr. Benjamin Carson, and at the age of 33, Ben was named head of pediatric neurosurgery at Johns Hopkins Hospital in Baltimore. In 1987 he became the first doctor to successfully separate Siamese twins joined at the back of the head. Since then he has pioneered other surgical procedures.

As a side note, Ben's mother only had a third grade education, and it turns out that she couldn't even read all those book reports Ben and his brother wrote for her. Amazing, isn't it?

The point of the story is that genuine confidence occurs when we take charge of our lives and move beyond our environment and heredity as the primary contributors to how we experience life. When Ben decided to commit himself to learning, he was slipping into the driver's seat. And for the rest of his life, he chose the direction and speed his vehicle would take.

Did Ben have walls to climb in his life? You bet — huge walls of poverty and racism and negativity. But because he had genuine confidence, he would climb wall after wall and have enough energy to tackle the next one.

Genuine confidence can help us scale walls that others wouldn't even dare to climb. But there's an even higher level of confidence than genuine confidence. I call it ultimate confidence, and it enables us to participate in all facets of the abundant life.

ULTIMATE CONFIDENCE

As you recall, the first level of confidence is *basic confidence*, that is, confidence that is shaped by our heredity and our experiences.

The second level is *genuine confidence*, which we develop only when we take control of our lives and determine the direction and speed of our lives, as was the case with Ben Carson.

The third and highest level of confidence is *ultimate confidence*, which is the level of confidence that King David possessed. David, you see, had taken control of his life and then surrendered it to a higher authority, his God. And because he had ultimate confidence, he was able to write, "Though a host encamp against me, yet I will be confident." This is why he was able to move ahead and meet the seemingly insurmountable giants that confronted him in life.

Rescued by Ultimate Confidence

On June 2, 1995, U. S. Air Force Captain Scott O'Grady was shot down over Bosnia as he was carrying out his mission to keep the skies clear of hostile planes bombing civilian targets.

O'Grady was flying in support of the lead plane when a missile hit his plane five miles above the surface of the earth. O'Grady ejected, but no one knew for six days whether he was dead or alive. When the missle hit, O'Grady thought he was going to die, and he immediately began praying, thanking God for a good life but asking not to die.

His prayers were answered when the ejection seat worked and the parachute landed him safely in enemy territory. As O'Grady hauled in his parachute, he could see troops coming from all directions to capture him. He ran into a dense forest and collapsed to the ground. For the next six days he remained as motionless as possible as one soldier after another passed by him, often within five feet. He spent those days in prayer and delving into his relationship with God.

After three days he ran out of water, and again, he began to pray. His prayers were answered again when it started to rain. O'Grady absorbed the rain water in a sponge and squeezed it into a bag to drink later. Several days later he ran out of water again, but he survived a while longer by squeezing the water out of his socks, which were still wet from the rain.

Captain Hanford was returning from his mission over Bosnia, and, though dangerously low on fuel, he searched the area where O'Grady had been shot down. O'Grady prayed on that sixth day that someone would discover he was alive. He turned on his radio and heard Captain Hanford's voice, and O'Grady was rescued within six hours of radio contact.

O'Grady states that during those six days in hiding, he knew he wasn't praying alone. He knew there were others praying for him in the United States and around the world. And he concluded his incredible story with these words: "Even though I was by myself, I was never alone." O'Grady had *ultimate confidence* because he knew that God is truly ever-present with us.

Scott O'Grady understood that quitting is NEVER an option, and he is living proof that individuals who have taken control of their lives and turn to God can proclaim as did King David, "Though a host encamp against me, yet I will be confident."

WHY ULTIMATE CONFIDENCE IS IMPORTANT

We need ultimate confidence today more than ever. It's obvious that we live in a world populated with people who lack a sense of meaning and purpose. As a result, there are a lot of angry, cynical malcontents who prefer seeing the cup of life as half-empty, as opposed to half-full. I call these negative people *antagonists*.

Antagonists personify the wise old saying, "Misery loves company." Like the Harpies in Greek mythology, the antagonists sit on the side line criticizing everything and everybody, including themselves. Antagonists especially love to attack everyone who is experiencing the abundant life, figuring if they can't be happy, no one else should be either.

When I think of why we must resist the attacks of antagonists, I'm reminded of the story of a man and his burro.

You Can't Be All Things to All People

It seems a father and son in ancient Egypt were preparing to go on a long journey. They packed up their burro and headed down the road.

They hadn't journeyed far when they came upon a group of young men who criticized the son for making his father walk. So the son placed his father upon the burro, and they continued on their way.

Before long they came upon another group who criticized the father for not allowing his son to ride with him on the burro, for after all, the burro was a beast of burden. So the son joined his father on the burro, and they continued down the road.

Within a few hours they came upon yet another group of critics. This group criticized the father and son for riding the burro in the hot sun. As a result, the father and son tied the burro's feet together, lashed it upside down to a pole, and carried the animal between them.

Soon the father and son came to a river with an old rickety bridge. As they got to the middle of it, the bridge gave way, and the three fell into the river below. The father and son swam to the banks and pulled themselves out. But the burro, with its legs still tied together, drowned.

The moral of the story is simply this: If you try to please everybody, you will lose your burro. There comes a time in our lives when we have to tune out the antagonists and follow our own advice. And that's why ultimate confidence is so crucial for those who wish to live the abundant life, for it's only through ultimate confidence that we can tune out the antagonists and remain centered and purposeful in our lives.

To Thine Own Self Be True

Ultimate confidence is essential to abundant living because we can't experience the abundant life without being true to ourselves and to others. After all, the only genuine relationships are based on honesty and integrity. Ultimate confidence comes to us when we take control of our own lives and then surrender them to a higher authority, our God.

When we have ultimate confidence, we come to an understanding that, regardless of what antagonists come our way, we will prevail. Without the concern for where we will end up in life ultimately, we are set free to truly live life in all of its richness and beauty, to face its many challenges. When we have an appropriate level of confidence and discover that we can't climb the wall, we don't despair because we're confident that we can always build a door.

ACHIEVING CONFIDENCE

What happens if we lack confidence in our lives, you may ask. To best answer that question, I'd like to tell you about a landmark experiment conducted on eight rhesus monkeys back in the 1950s.

The monkeys were divided into four pairs, and each of the monkeys was administered electric shocks at the same time and also at periodic intervals. One monkey in each pair, however, could prevent the electric shock by simply flicking off a switch when a light flashed on.

After a short time, four of the eight monkeys developed ulcers and lesions and died. Now, which four monkeys do you think died? The ones who didn't have access to a switch and couldn't turn off the shock? Or the ones who could turn off the shock when the light came on?

The answer may surprise you. The monkeys who COULD turn off the electric shocks were the ones who died! The researchers concluded that the electric shocks didn't kill the monkeys. *Their anxiety killed them!*

147

Lack of Confidence Could Be Fatal

I think this study is fascinating because it bears out what I've been saying. You see, the monkeys who had access to the switch could control their fate, but they lacked confidence. If they were totally confident they could avoid the pain of an electrical shock by the flick of a switch, their anxiety level would drop to normal levels.

But they weren't confident. So they worried. They fretted. They were kept in a constant state of anxiety, and that anxiety — "maybe I'm in control, maybe I'm not" — drove them to an early grave.

The other monkeys, on the other hand, resigned themselves to the fact that they'd experience some pain now and then. They didn't have any expectations of being able to control their fates, so they just took their shocks and went on with their lives.

I see the same thing happening to people in our world as happened to the dead monkeys — so many people are riddled with anxiety that it's driving them to an early grave. Why? Because, like the monkeys, they sense they have some control, but they lack ultimate confidence. As a result, they live in a constant state of anxiety, thinking they're IN CONTROL one minute, OUT OF CONTROL the next. And the insecurity and uncertainty are driving them crazy!

Never Too Old to Achieve Ultimate Confidence

Diogenes was the ancient philosopher who walked around Athens carrying a lantern in broad daylight looking for an honest man. He was an unconventional thinker for the time because he believed that the key to happiness is found within and that the simplest life is the best.

Even in old age he remained very active, so much so that one of his disciples encouraged him to slow down.

"I know that many believe that old age is a time to take it easy," Diogenes responded. "I compare it to a relay race in which I am the last runner. Would you have me slow down before the finish line?"

The same can be said for all of us. It's never too late to develop ultimate confidence, no matter what your age, for why would anyone want to slow down just before the finish line? Confidence, you see, is something that belongs to people of every age and station in life.

REVIEW

Confidence is the belief in our own ability to negotiate the walls in our lives. There are three levels of confidence:
1) Basic confidence
2) Genuine confidence
3) Ultimate confidence

Basic confidence

Basic confidence comes to us as the consequence of our experiences in life. When we have positive experiences, our basic confidence grows. On the other hand, when we have negative experiences, our confidence wanes. Hence, our basic confidence can continually be in a state of flux, inasmuch as life has both its ups and downs.

Genuine confidence

Genuine confidence comes to us as we take control of our own lives. We exhibit genuine confidence when we recognize that our experiences aren't left up to chance and that we, in large part, can determine the course we take in life.

Ultimate confidence

Ultimate confidence comes to us when we take control of our own lives and then surrender ourselves to a higher authority, our God. In this case, we come to understand that regardless of what antagonists come our way, our destiny is ensured through the goodness and grace of God. Without the concern for where we will end up in life, we're set free to truly live life in all of its richness and beauty and to face its many challenges.

Achieving confidence

Unless we have ultimate confidence, we will always exist in varying states of anxiety. As a result, the anxiety of thinking we are IN CONTROL one minute, and then thinking we're OUT OF CONTROL the next is taking a toll on our physical and mental health. Today, more than ever, we need ultimate confidence in order to become centered in the abundant life.

CONCLUSION

~

What Is Your Message to the World?

When one door of happiness closes, another opens;
but often we look so long at the closed door that we
do not see the one that has opened before us.
— Helen Keller

Mahatma Gandhi, the great Indian leader, was boarding a train to take him to yet another protest that would eventually lead to India's independence from British rule.

As Gandhi was turning to enter the passenger cabin, a young reporter ran alongside the train and shouted, "Sir, what is your message to the people?"

Gandhi paused for a moment before answering calmly, *"My life is my message."*

A Message of Love and Justice

Gandhi was a very wise and courageous man, and I think his reply on the spur of the moment captures the essence of what I hope you have learned from reading this book.

Certainly Gandhi's life sent a message of integrity ... justice ... love ... and an unbreakable determination to climb the walls and open the doors to a life of abundance not only for himself, but for all the oppressed people in the world.

Just look at some of the walls Gandhi had to negotiate in his life. A dedicated pacifist, Gandhi fought for justice by organizing the first massive sit-ins and nonviolent strikes.

He drew attention to his causes with hunger strikes, often going months without food.

And he openly defied India's rigid caste system by proclaiming that the lowest caste in India, the "untouchables," were just as worthy as the highest caste. As an historical footnote, 50 years after India received its independence from England, the world's largest democracy elected a member of the untouchables caste as president, an achievement that would have been unthinkable during Gandhi's life.

What Is Your Message?

Like Gandhi, I believe with all my heart that your life is your message. And I believe each of us — me, you, your best friend, and yes, even your worst enemy — has a message to witness to the world.

What message is your life sending to your spouse? To your children? To your friends and neighbors? To the family of man? To the world at large? To God?

Is your life sending a message that says, *I can do this ... I'll keep climbing until I'm at the top ... I'll find a way ...* and *My life is a model of love and integrity?*

Or is your life sending a message that says, *I'm a quitter ... I can't do this ... Life is too hard ...* and *I give up?*

My friend, God didn't create you to send a message of failure and defeat. You were born to send a message of triumph and abundance.

Quitting Is NEVER an Option!

Time and again the story is the same. The secret to success is simply getting up one more time than you fall down.

Whether you are like Scott O'Grady, who was shot down over Bosnia in the prime of his life. Or whether you are like Col. Sanders, who was starting a new business when everyone else his age was retired — you, too, CAN meet the challenges before you!

You, too, CAN actualize your potential!

You, too, CAN seize a life of abundance!

You, too, CAN climb the walls of adversity and build the doors through your challenges until the world hears your message loud and clear:

I didn't quit — I TRIUMPHED!